The Shakespeare Factory
Moon River: The Deal
David

Seren Drama

Dannie Abse: *The View from Row G*
Lucinda Coxon: *Waiting at the Water's Edge*
Greg Cullen: *Mary Morgan/Tarzanne/Frida and Diego*
Peter Lloyd: *The Scam*
Edward Thomas: *Three Plays*
Gwyn Thomas: *Three Plays*
Charles Way: *Three Plays*

Phil Clark (ed): *Act One Wales*

DIC EDWARDS
The Shakespeare Factory
Moon River: The Deal
David

seren

seren
is the book imprint of
Poetry Wales Press Ltd
Wyndham Street, Bridgend, Wales

ISBN 1-85411-224-2

A CIP record for this title is available from
the British Library

*The publisher works with the financial assistance of the
Arts Council of Wales*

Cover: Andy Dark

Printed in Palatino by CPD Wales

Contents

For Natalie

The Shakespeare Factory

Notes to the Original Production

The Shakespeare Factory was commissioned by Spectacle Theatre with support from the Arts Council of Wales. This play was first performed on September 13, 1993 at Cyfarthfa High School, Merthyr Tydfil.

Directed by	Steve Davis
Designed by	Janis Hart
Stage Manager	Dewi Garrow-Smith

Cast

Jack Cash (Factory Shop-Steward)
(Brendan Charleson)

Gillian Brutus (Factory Manager)/Jennifer/Mechanical
(Anna Garth)

Jane/ Mechanical
(Sian Rivers)

Peter/Gov't Officer/Mechanical/Politician
(Alan Grice)

PROLOGUE

ALL: We have made a play for you from Shakespeare
to try and help to make a few things clear
not least that his plays work as magic'lly
today as in those days when tragic'lly
told tales were most in fashion. Plays are plays!
They play as in a game you play to change
the order of a world mostly arranged
for you by others like politicians,
who may say "learn!" yet cut books; musicians
have strings stolen, but imagination,
which you own, is yours for the creation
of a world in which you can thrive. This world
is the world his poet's mind unfurled.
Illusion IS real but alternative
it can free you from the conservative!

So imagine a factory away
in a woods where our waiting dreams may play.
In this factory, videos are made
of his plays, each ten minutes long when played:
merely the plots that made his plays a hit
so that in the curriculum they'll fit!
These are the days of ripe honeysuckle
of full-fruited sun and wild eglantine
when love like a ring slipped on a knuckle
sweats in the heat of Summer's festive shine.
These are the day times of Radio One
air-waved endlessly from hour to hour
with rock-song and ballads for loving young
commingling their limbs in leafy bower!
And these are the days of the factory:

9

Act One
SCENE ONE

GILLIAN: What was wrong with the *Julius Caesar*?

GOVERN-
MENT
OFFICER: It was too long!

GILLIAN: [*with disbelief*] Too long at ten minutes?!

G.O.: We want them cut....

GILLIAN: Cut?

G.O.: This is what I've come to tell you.

GILLIAN: You can't be serious!

G.O.: You're being reactionary, Ms Brutus. Let's not hold out for tradition. Tradition is not a living thing.

GILLIAN: Who's talking about tradition? I want Shakespeare to live for the kids. You want us to cut the videos from ten minutes to five. That's not some spicy anti-traditional stance, that's slitting the throat of an already haemorrhaging playwright!

G.O.: As a government we have a mandate: to cut the running times of the Shakespeare! Or maybe you think that our commitments are something we can be whimsical about?

GILLIAN: But you want to make the cuts to save money,

that's all! It doesn't matter whether the kids' understanding of Shakespeare suffers. Isn't that it?

G.O.: You do as we say. We say five minutes, you do five minutes. The absolute hard fact is that Shakespeare does not affect the lives of ordinary people: they're a bit like the Roman mob. And so even five minutes is probably wasted on them. Shakespeare wrote about EXTRAordinary people and these we cater for separately.

GILLIAN: I suppose you mean those children who go to private schools or schools for the better off?

G.O.: You have your instructions! [*suddenly calmer*] Look, Ms Brutus, I'm sorry. It's got nothing to do with me. I work for the government. I take instructions too, which I pass on.

GILLIAN: It's clear you don't have children of your own.

G.O.: [*to audience*] I'm putting up with her outrageous familiarity because, I have to say, I have growing in me a soft spot for Ms Brutus like the centre of a very hot Mount Etna! [*to GILLIAN*] No, I don't have children. But even if I did it wouldn't change my position. I AM a government officer. The next video, the *Romeo and Juliet* will have to be ready by the 20th of June. I'll be along to pick it up. In person.

GILLIAN: How curious.

G.O.: Not at all. It's simply that I see it as my duty to personally take delivery of this particular...

GILLIAN: I don't mean that, I meant that the 20th of June is Mid-Summer Night's Eve!

G.O.: The relevance escapes me!

GILLIAN: And that is not surprising! Thank you.

[*GILLIAN offers her hand for the GOVERNMENT*

11

OFFICER to shake. He seems a little confused, then shakes it. He leaves. GILLIAN paces for a moment in worried thought. She calls off:]

GILLIAN: Jack!

[JACK CASH, the factory shop steward, comes on.]

GILLIAN: Oh, Jack!

[She suddenly checks herself.]

CASH: What's the matter? What did he want?

GILLIAN: They're reducing the running time of the videos. They're CUTTING it from ten minutes to five.

CASH: But why?

GILLIAN: To save money!

CASH: I can't believe it! What next! Perhaps they'll have a Nazi bonfire of books. When are we going to fight back against this?

GILLIAN: He compared the children with the Roman mob! He said that Shakespeare cannot affect the lives of ordinary people.

CASH: *[very angrily]* Cannot affect the lives of ordinary people! Well I think we should show him, Gillian. This government bestrides the narrow world as though it were a Colossus because we behave like petty men! We walk under its huge legs and creep about to find ourselves dishonourable positions! Factory Managers! *[points at GILLIAN]* Foreman! Shop-stewards! We've become government agents — doing its dirty work!

GILLIAN: Hang on, Jack. This is a democracy!

CASH: It's got nothing to do with democracy. The name of Shakespeare is used as previous generations have used the name of God! To strike fear into the hearts of children! They're more easily controlled when they're fearful in this way. I don't want to

12

be a part of this cynicism, Gillian. If there is democracy then it's founded on the best values of theatre. The arena! Where things are debated! If we cut Shakespeare down to five minutes we may as well cut their right to vote when they're old enough. Or let them vote for Mickey Mouse!

GILLIAN: But do you think that people are ever masters of their own fate?

CASH: Yes!

GILLIAN: Well, they're not. And the fault, dear Jack, is not in our stars but in ourselves that we are underlings.

CASH: So are we always to be told: What dost thou with thy best apparel on? We'll tell you when you can have a party. And we'll tell you how much Shakespeare and how much democracy you get. If people were never to be masters of their own fate, why educate them?

GILLIAN: [*importantly*] I am surprised. They say Jack Cash loves no plays, hears no music and smiles in such a sort as if he mock'd himself. That he loves only politics. So what's all this about theatre?

CASH: I am an actor. And as as actor I deal in irony. And a great irony, Gillian, is to see you defend the government's position!

GILLIAN: What choice do I have? They make the laws! The rules!

[*CASH lets out a cry of despair. He begins to go.*]

GILLIAN: Jack, don't cause any trouble on the shop floor.

CASH: *We* have to study the plays. *We* have to know the plays. *We* are ordinary people, and *we* deserve something better than five minutes. *We* should be doing longer, not shorter versions. Then we would show just how deeply Shakespeare could affect even ordinary people.

GILLIAN: You don't know your own workers, Jack. They won't be interested. They're politically asleep and, pitifully, with brain and expectation as sadly pitted as a Dutch elm. Tell them five minutes and they'll immediately reason that that's less work than ten.

CASH: Perhaps. But they'll soon discover just how paradoxical that is. Five minutes will mean a lot more REAL work. What is condensed for the classroom will be made proportionately more intense for us. You have to work at betrayal. [*as he goes*] We should do a full-length film!

GILLIAN: [*shouting after him*] We couldn't do that. It would be an act of... subversion. We are not empowered in our lives this way. [*to audience*] I love him! I love Jack Cash. And yet all I can talk with him about are unloving things! If I let my love for Jack instruct me in what I do, I must turn against the government and lose my job. But if I do my job, I stand to lose all hopes of having Jack! Oh, unhappy me! I wish some magical, mystical thing like a thought-wave from Shakespeare's mind could come and change my life!

SCENE TWO

[*The Shopfloor. PETER is front of stage speaking to the audience. At the back, JANE and JENNIFER pace, with* Romeo and Juliet *text in hand, learning lines. Music to reflect action.*]

PETER: Jack Cash spends hours in a day with Gillian Brutus! He loves her, I'm sure. But *I* love her! Love is a smoke raised with the fume of sighs or in my case imagined sighs and I am choking in a fog! And when I think of him with her, how I would be happy if they were to choke on it! I'm Peter. I live in those blessed places where the effervescence of Gillian's scent has fallen. She comes to me through keyholes and fainting doors. When she passes I breathe deep the perfume of her argument.

JENNIFER: Peter!

PETER: What!

JENNIFER: The bud is bit with an envious worm!

[*PETER goes off a little angrily.*]

JENNIFER: (*to audience*) I love Peter. Spread thy close curtain, love-performing night, that Peter leap into these arms. But who does HE love? Not Jane?

[*JENNIFER walks off, perplexed. JANE comes to the front of the stage.*]

JANE: I think I love Jack! Jack Cash, my Union Shop Steward; my master; my balladeer in a ghetto blaster! But does Jack love me? Is the music of his night played on my recorder? Isn't it strange how the more love is showed the less affection is returned! If I told Jack I loved him he would strut like Iago on a black man's shadow, cock-a-hoop and I had un-hooped a cock! But were I reticent and retiring he would be by moonlight at my window singing. [*pause*] Oh, but I know men! I know how, with feigning voice they sing verses of feigning love!

[*JACK CASH comes on.*]

CASH: This is how it is.

[*JANE gasps.*]

JANE: He comes like thunder, lightning and all the portents of the perilously portalled night!

15

CASH: The *Caesar* video was too long at ten minutes. They will say, I know, that an attention span of five minutes is the limit for today's kids. That's rubbish. It's true if the content of what is shown is trivial or unconcerning — concerning them, like news reports made up of sound bites to trigger programmed responses. This is what they want to do to Shakespeare; turn the play into a news report, sound bite. [*As though doing a news report:*] Today the seemingly endless feud between the Capulets and the Montagues, two of Verona's top families, came to a sad if not tragic end when Romeo Montague and Juliet Capulet committed suicide in a crypt near the town. Friar Lawrence, who found the bodies, says it was all a tragic mistake. Juliet had taken a potion to feign death so that she wouldn't have to marry her fiancé, Paris, because she'd fallen in love with Romeo. Romeo found her and believing her dead, killed himself. Juliet, on waking, found Romeo's body then killed herself. Police say foul play is not suspected.

JENNIFER: What are you getting at, Jack?

CASH: They want the *Romeo and Juliet* video to be five minutes.

[*Cheers.*]

CASH: You're crazy!

PETER: No! we'll get paid the same for doing less!

CASH: Well, let me tell you, you will actually do much more!

JANE: How, Jack? That doesn't make sense.

CASH: Well, we could do the basic plot; A comes on, B goes off, gets C who poisons A in what, two minutes, but it's in the three minutes that we have left that we have to show our understanding of

Shakespeare. That's obviously much harder to do than if you've got eight minutes.

PETER: Let me get this straight. You're arguing that we should do the ten and not the five?

CASH: Yes!

PETER: I'll go on strike!

CASH: Against what?

PETER: Against you!

CASH: You can't go on strike against me, I'm your Shop Steward. You can't go on strike against your Union!

JENNIFER: I think he's got a point there, Peter, even though I agree with you.

PETER: You'd join me on strike?

JENNIFER: Of course I would!

JANE: This is stupid!

JENNIFER: You're only saying that because you love Jack!

JANE: I'm not! I've got my doubts but we've got to be sensible!

CASH: It boils down to this: you can't take flesh off what is already a skeleton. There's no easy way. If you think there is you'll find yourselves working harder. You will have to become so familiar with the texts that you will need to wear them as you wear your underclothes!

JENNIFER: I wouldn't mind if they were Peter's!

JANE: Jenny! Stop demeaning yourself!

PETER: If I didn't know that the FABRIC of these dramas is more dramatic than even an Elizabethan codpiece I would not have the good sense to know that our best interests lie in doing what they want. There's nothing we can do against it.

JANE: Star-crossed workers! We're in the hands of fate!

PETER: It's not a question of fate! It's what the government wants and governments are democratically elected.

CASH: But the government is behaving like a dictator. This democracy has become despotism by another name. I think we should follow the example of those who conspired against Caesar.

PETER: Be real! Anyway, at least we've got a job!

CASH: We'd be better off defying them. Produce a film-length video of *A Midsummer Night's Dream*. At least then we'd have something of value with which to make a stand against the vandalism of this government. Something that would be a symbol.

OTHERS: No!

JENNIFER: You couldn't do it without Gillian and Gillian won't put our jobs at risk for something that your ordinary people won't be allowed to see.

[*Silence.*]

CASH: All right. Shall we spend the rest of the day looking at the play and start tomorrow?

OTHERS: O.K. Yes. Sure. See ya.

[*OTHERS go. CASH is alone. JANE can be seen listening.*]

CASH: I'm worried. This age is one where wisdom which spurns facile judgement is itself spurned. By laziness. The metaphor of the day is of the banker collecting interest. A lazy act which produces nothing of great value but that which can seem to be worth a lot in a little age: money. In this age the value of a thing made is not measured by the work and commitment that built it but by how much it costs. But such an age is doomed. It is doomed because we are men and women. We grow when the value of our work grows. But when that work is devalued so that the usurer may make his interest, we perish. Five minute Shakespeares will not save us. They will simply provide those who want to shut us down with their reason for doing so. This is not adapting wisely to the times, it's the prelude to the executioner's busiest hour.

[*JANE comes on.*]

JANE: Jack!

[*CASH gasps.*]

CASH: You nearly gave me a heart attack!

JANE: Oh Jack, I wish I could!

CASH: Jane!

JANE: Jack! [*pause*] Jack!

CASH: What?

[*Pause.*]

JANE: I... take me out tonight. Let's get away from all this. It's driving you mad.

CASH: What do you mean?

JANE: We're young, Jack. Even if they close the factory down we can still get other work!

CASH: Not in the long run. Not if people think like you.

JANE: Time moves on! Old desire doth in his death bed lie, and young affection gapes to be his heir!

[*JANE holds onto CASH.*]

CASH: Is love and sex all you people can think of! God, Jane! If all poetry had to do was to be beautiful and if all we needed to achieve beauty was love poetry then your words might be perfect. But I actually think there's something claustrophobic about the purely beautiful. There's some kind of truth missing.

[*JANE pulls away, hurt.*]

JANE: Thank you, Jack. I was quoting from the play. And it's better than the bitterness you share with your wall.

CASH: What?

JANE: I heard you!

CASH: You heard me?

JANE: Yes, I was listening. Ranting on. Like a madman.

CASH: [*outraged*] But that was a soliloquy!

[*He suddenly holds JANE and shakes her.*]

CASH: A soliloquy!

JANE: Stop it, Jack!

[*He stops.*]

CASH: A soliloquy is a private thing between the character giving it and the audience!

JANE: Private?!

CASH: It belongs to the audience in a way that a public speech between character and character cannot. It brings theatre directly into the mind of the audience. It's like a silence with whispers. Like a secret told. It makes the audience... responsible. Morally involved! You've let them off the hook by spying! Do you know what your world is Jane, with your love intrigues?

JANE: Intrigues!

CASH: A world of dreams! I see Queen Mab hath been

with you. She is the faeries' midwife and she comes in shape no bigger than an agate stone on the forefinger of an alderman, drawn with a little team of atomies, athwart men's noses as they lie asleep!

JANE: [*tearfully*] Very clever, Jack, quoting Mercutio at me. I hate you!

[*She turns away from him.*]

CASH: Your lovers' world is a world of illusion! It's not like that. The real world. This world of dying industry and shrinking expectation. Yours is a world of dreams. The sweet dying potions of the faeries' midwife!

JANE: But our world IS a world of illusion! You're too interested in your petty power politics to see where our real power lies.

CASH: What do you mean?

JANE: The theatre is a world of illusion. The fairy's midwife or Puck in *Midsummer Night's Dream* are the way Shakespeare describes that little imp of imagination that exists in all of us. That imagination that gives us our power. Look at *Romeo and Juliet*. Don't you think it is a very convincing play?

[*CASH deep in thought, Jane begins to wrap herself around him.*]

CASH: Yes.

JANE: Why?

CASH: What?

JANE: Why?

CASH: Well...

JANE: Because moments of love are very important in the theatre: they are the most INTENSE illusion of a world which is ALL illusion! And you may complain that we only talk of love and not politics but love, Jack, is the politics of the heart.

CASH: [*Ecstatically, as JANE puts hand between his legs.*] Yes! [*He turns to JANE as if coming out of a dream.*] No! Jane. [*He jumps up, JANE gasps hopelessly and runs off.*]

Act Two
SCENE ONE

[Morning. All are assembled ready for a warm-up.]

CASH: O.K., beginning with me, we'll go round; a line each to build up the plot. Right, two families, Montagues and Capulets, hate each other...

JANE: In Verona.

CASH: What?

JANE: The play is set in Verona!

[Pause.]

CASH: O.K. Start again. Two families, in Verona, Montagues and Capulets, hate each other and are always fighting.

JANE: Aeschelus, Prince of Verona, is tired of the brawling and threatens them with their lives if they don't stop.

PETER: Romeo Montague is in love with...

JENNIFER: *[enthusiastically]* Rosaline!

CASH: BUT, Romeo goes disguised to a Capulet ball and falls in love with...

JANE: *[indifferently]* Juliet.

PETER: My only love sprang from my only hate.

JANE: What?

PETER: That's what she said.

CASH: Yes, but stick to telling the plot!

JENNIFER: Where were we?

CASH: They plan to marry secretly. Come on, quicker!

PETER: Why quicker? You're doing this just to win your point but it won't prove your argument!

CASH: For God's sake, Peter! It's a warm-up! Would you prefer the bean bag?

JENNIFER
& JANE: No, no!

CASH: O.K., from the top! Let's start again. Two families, Montagues and Capulets, IN VERONA, hate each other and are always fighting...

JANE: Aeschelus, Prince of Verona, is tired of the brawling and threatens to execute them if they don't stop.

PETER: Romeo Montague is in love with...

JENNIFER: Me, O, God, sorry: Rosaline.

CASH: But Romeo goes disguised to a Capulet ball and falls in love with...

JANE: Juliet.

JENNIFER: Romeo goes to Friar Lawrence who says he'll help him...

CASH: And Juliet's Nurse will help her.

JANE: Nurse gets message; tells Juliet to go to Friar Lawrence's cell.

PETER: She goes. Meanwhile, in the street, Tybalt, a Capulet, challenges Romeo.

JENNIFER: Romeo refuses to fight so Tybalt kills Mercutio and then...

CASH: Romeo kills Tybalt which means....

JANE: Romeo will be banished, Friar Lawrence AD-VISES Romeo to go to comfort the sad Juliet, but be gone...

PETER: By the break of day.

JENNIFER: Juliet's parents want her to marry Paris, and arrange it.

CASH: Romeo is banished to Mantua. Meanwhile, Friar Lawrence...

JANE: Gives Juliet a drug which will make it look as if she's dead. He sends a letter...

PETER: To Romeo but the letter gets lost. Romeo hears that Juliet is dead and...

JENNIFER: Rushes back to Verona and finds Juliet apparently dead in Friar Lawrence's cell.

CASH: Romeo poisons himself in his grief.

JANE: Juliet wakes and finding Romeo dead, kills herself.

PETER: The warring houses come together and stop fighting.

CASH: Good. So, what do we leave in and what do we leave out to get our five minutes?

PETER: Well, isn't the play about the relationship between young people and adults? The young paying for the crimes of their elders.

JENNIFER: Can we sit down?

JANE: Yes!

            [*They sit. JANE sits close to CASH. JENNIFER sits too close to PETER. He seems uncomfortable.*]

JANE: It's about a feud and a pair of star-crossed lovers who bring reconciliation to the families with their deaths. What's so true about it is... Juliet's love for Romeo.

JENNIFER: We know that, Jane.

JANE: No, I feel as if I understand it. It's like: children live in society and are always told to be law-takers but are never allowed to make decisions about their own lives: "YOU will marry Paris"!

PETER: But they're told to be law-takers, Jane, because when they grow they'll be law-takers. That's the truth of it.

JANE: But if we live in a democracy... well, in a democracy THE PEOPLE make the laws, so how are the children to grow up to be law-makers if they're told only that they will always be law-takers.

CASH: Do you think we're getting a little away from the point?

JENNIFER: Yes, Verona wasn't a democracy, Jane.

JANE: O.K., but do you think it's different here, in this country? We are a democracy but how many of our children will think it worthwhile even to VOTE let alone become law-makers?

CASH: This common body, like to a vagabond flag upon the stream goes to and back LACKEYING the varying tide, to rot itself with motion.

JANE: What's that?

CASH: Caesar, from *Anthony and Cleopatra*.

JANE: Julius?

CASH: Oh, no, Augustus. Known as Octavian. The role of ordinary people in politics is an important element in Shakespeare. But why do you think it's important?

JANE: I think it's what the play is about. These two young people who only want to love, die because of the fighting of the law-makers. But the action that matters takes place in Friar Lawrence's cell. What goes on in the street, the feuding, is trivial by comparison. And really trivial. And that's what's so tragic. I think the play is about claustrophobia.

PETER: So you don't think it's a play about fate?

JANE: No, no, it's much too modern for that. It's not a play about feuding. It's a tragedy about two lovers in which murder is only one of the things, one of the dramatic elements, which separates them. I think they transcend the feuding just as Hamlet transcends the wars in that play.

JENNIFER: That's all very well, Jane, but you said that the parents are the law-makers but they're not. The Prince is.

CASH: But Shakespeare lived in a monarchy and I'm sure he felt obliged to set his play in a monarchy, that's all.

JENNIFER: That's not fair! Is it about...?

CASH: What you're saying is that if Romeo and Juliet had lived they would have grown up to be like their parents. Driven not by the forces of justice but by sectarianism. But that's not the play. In the play right up until almost the last moment they could have lived and grown to be old, but they don't. They die in this little cold cell. That's what we have to deal with. True, outside the boundaries of that cell in the world of the Capulets and the Montagues, the IRA and the UDA or the Serbs and the Croats and the Bosnian Moslems, Shakespeare presents a huge historical perspective, but that's not the essence of the play.

JENNIFER: [bemused] So you agree with Jane?

CASH: Well, we couldn't put that kind of historical sweep into five minutes even if we had to. What Jane has argued shows that we don't have to. I think the heart of the story does beat in that small cold cell. [*pause*] Shall we spend some time working on this idea?

SCENE TWO

[*The same. Later. JANE is on the floor crying. The others look perplexed.*]

CASH: Jane, remember what you said about the theatre being a world of illusion. Come on.

JANE: The trouble with talking about these things as illusion in the way you do is that it makes the lovers seem unreal in their passion. But this story is REAL!

[*PETER hugs JANE to comfort her.*]

PETER: Jane, Jane!

JENNIFER: Why don't you call her Juliet?

CASH: Jennifer! [*shirtily*] I'm sorry, Jane. I don't think I understand what you mean.

JANE: I mean that this so called illusory world, making PICTURES with our acting, with our bodies, is not so illusory, it's real enough for me! I know what it's all about. In that cell are two people who are using their IMAGINATION to make a world that challenges the corrupt old world of their parents. It's the world that shuts them into that little cell but they fight back with their love. Love becomes their politics. It's much more serious than a frivolous love affair. Their lives hang on the outcome of their love.

[*PETER holds onto her as they kneel.*]

JANE: [*aside*] I am finding the touch of Peter's trembling fingers on my distress, setting my arguments to trembling. How strongly do I love Jack with his

28

emotionless, cold fingers on my heart?

[*as JULIET*]
Spread thy close curtain, love-performing night,
    that runaways' eyes may wink, and Romeo
    leap to these arms, untalk'd of and unseen.
    Lovers can see to do their amorous rites
    by their own beauties; or if love be blind,
    it best agrees with night. Come, civil night,
    thou sober-suited matron, all in black,
    and learn me how to lose a winning match,
    play'd for a pair of stainless maidenhoods;
    hood my unmann'd blood, bating in my cheeks,
    with my black mantle, till strange love grows
                            bold,
    think true love acted simple modesty.

PETER: I understand what she feels! That was good, Jane.
          You became her!

          [*He holds her closer.*]

JANE: She is fourteen! She is about to love someone
          COMPLETELY for the first time. I think... I think
          there's the anticipation of suicide in this.

CASH: How?

JANE: Because she is drawn to conclude that she needs
          to be hooded, hidden by the night. As though she
          was calling on the clowns of claustrophobia.

PETER: And I became her Christ and her Judas, her night
          and her day, I will save her and I will murder her.
          We need this image.

          [*PETER enfolds her as though he were a cage around
          her. JANE looks vulnerable and holds onto him. While
          CASH speaks, PETER and JANE talk quietly to each
          other, experimenting with positions.*]

CASH: [*to Audience*] The immediacy of love puzzled the
          Elizabethans like any other phenomenon of
          nature. These [*about PETER and JANE*] flashes of
          recognition or of LOVE have special importance

in the theatre: they are the most intense illusion of a world which is all illusion. This is a very convincing play! [*As though he'd only just discovered it.*] I am in love with Jane! And he is curled around her like Frank Sinatra's tongue around a love song! Oh, Peter is such a smoothie! Look how he leans against her neck like a thief's ladder against an unalarmed, virgin wall.

JENNIFER: I'm bored!

CASH: [*still to audience*] And look how she swallows his words like a child gorging on chips!

JENNIFER: If it's all taking place in the cell, what's the nurse supposed to do?

PETER: [*testily*] Look, Jennifer, you're out there, looking in. You should be able to see how you fit!

JENNIFER: Fit! Where? You're like ivy round a drainpipe!

CASH: And, as in old Latin poetry, the ivy that destroys the tree was a metaphor for death.

PETER: [*seeing their antagonism*] Well, it fits then, doesn't it?

[*JENNIFER gets down by them and forces herself between them.*]

JENNIFER: [*with a very gossipy, 'common' accent*] Where was I? Oh yes, like I says:

'Tis since the earthquake now eleven years;
And she was wean'd — I never shall forget it —
Juliet, of course is what I'm talking about,
   Of all the days of the year, upon that day;
For I had then laid wormwood to my dug,
Sitting in the sun under the dove-house wall;
   My lord and you were then at Mantua,
   Nay, I do bear a brain. But as I said,
When it did taste the wormwood on the nipple
Of my dug [*she holds her breast*], and felt it bitter,

>   pretty fool,
> To see it tetchy, and fall out with the dug!

[*JENNIFER laughs.*]

PETER: That doesn't mean anything here!

JENNIFER: Well, I think it puts an appropriate bitter note amongst all this silly sweetness!

[*PETER gets up angrily.*]

PETER: We can't do it if people start getting petty!

CASH: No one's getting petty! THAT would be most IN-appropriate.

[*He takes on a 'fighting' pose and circles PETER.*]

PETER: So what now?

CASH: Well, come on! You're the cool, smooth dude, Pretty Romeo!

[*CASH goads PETER giving him a poke now and again.*]

JANE: Leave it out, Jack!

CASH: Leave it out? Shut it, sister!

PETER: You leave it out, Cash!

CASH: Tybalt.

PETER: [*sceptically*] Oh, yes!

[*JANE gets up.*]

JANE: Why are you talking to me like that?

[*PETER accidentally hits CASH. They fight. The women complain. CASH ends up on top of PETER and is about to hit him.*]

JENNIFER
& JANE: Stop!

CASH: [*to Audience*] What am I doing? Is this real?

[*He stops, gets up and begins to go off.*]

CASH: It can't be done! We can't do this by under-standing it. We'll just do the five-minute version, O.K.?

[*He goes.*]

SCENE THREE

[*The company cast the five minute version.*]

CASH: I'll be Narrator.

OTHERS: I'll be Romeo, I'll be Balthazaar, etc., etc.

CASH: In order to get it down to five minutes, we'll have to cut the secondary actions and deal with critical, climactic action. O.K.?

OTHERS: O.K.

[*The five minute version should be acted out with a lot of energy and humour, even some clowning.*]

CASH: [*as Narrator*] Right: long shot, slow zoom in on Romeo in the street in Mantua as his friend Balthazaar runs up to him.

ROMEO: News from Verona! How now, Balthazaar! How fares my Juliet?

BALTH-
AZAAR: Her body sleeps in Capulet's monument, and her immortal-part with Angels lives.

ROMEO: Is it e'en so? Then I deny you stars! Thou knowst my lodging, get me ink and papers, and hire post horses, I will hence tonight. Hast thou no letter to me from the Friar?

BALTH-
AZAAR: No, my good lord.

ROMEO: No matter, get thee gone. [*He goes.*] Well, Juliet, I will lie with thee tonight.

NARRATOR: Close-up of Romeo leaving the Apothecary, with poison, is met by Balthazaar with horses and mounting, they depart for Verona. Fade — shot of Friary, we see Friar Lawrence receive news that his letter has not reached Romeo, and not knowing Romeo has already left, says he will write again to him in Mantua. Wide shot of churchyard tracking back to reveal Capulet's Tomb. Establishing shot of Juliet's body. Shot of Paris approaching tomb.

PARIS: Sweet flower, with flowers thy bridal bed I strew, Oh! Woe! Thy canopy is dust and stones.

NARRATOR: A page hears someone and whistles in warning.

PARIS: What cursed foot wanders this way tonight to cross my obsequies and true love's rite?

NARRATOR: Romeo enters the tombs to find Paris in grief. He spins round full face to camera.

PARIS: Stop thy unhallowed toil, vile Montague. Can vengeance be pursued further than death? Condemned villain, I do apprehend thee. Obey, and go with me for thou must die.

ROMEO: I must indeed, and therefore came I hither. I beseech thee, you put not another sin upon my head by urging me to fury.

PARIS: I do defy thy conjurations and apprehend thee for a felon here.

ROMEO: Wilt thou provoke me, then have at thee. [*They fight — PARIS dies.*] Oh! My love! My wife! Death, that hath suck'd the honey of thy breath, hath had no power yet upon thy beauty. Eyes, look your last, arms take your last embrace! And lips, oh, you, the doors of breath seal with a righteous kiss, a dateless bargain to engrossing death! — [*He drinks.*] Oh, true apothecary! Thy drugs are quick. Thus with a kiss, *I* die. [*And so he does.*]

NARRATOR: Camera pans back to tomb entrance. We see Friar Lawrence hurrying in and discovering the bodies of Romeo and Paris.

FRIAR: Romeo! Oh! Pale, who else! What! Paris too? And steeped in blood? — The lady stirs. [*JULIET wakes.*]

JULIET: Oh comfortable Friar! Where is my Lord?

FRIAR: Lady, come from the nest of death, contagion and unnatural sleep. Thy husband in thy bosom there lies dead, and Paris too, come. Stay not to question, for the watch is coming. Come, go, good Juliet.

JULIET: Go, get thee hence, for I will not away. [*Exit FRIAR LAWRENCE.*]

[*JULIET kisses ROMEO'S dead lips.*]

JULIET: Oh, happy dagger! This is thy sheath, there rust and let me die! [*She dies.*]

NARRATOR: Wide shot. The watch arrive, and discover the bodies and raise the alarm.

WATCH: What ho? Alarm! Alarm!

NARRATOR: The Prince arrives and addresses both houses.

PRINCE: Where be these enemies? Capulet! Montague! See what a scourge is laid upon your hate, that heaven finds means to kill your joys with love.

NARRATOR:The warring houses come together and stop fighting.

PRINCE: A glooming peace this morning with it brings. The sun for sorrow will not show his head. Go hence, to have mere talk of these sad things. Some shall be pardoned and some punished. For never was a story of more woe, than this of Romeo and Juliet-O.

[The tensions that have come out of the intensity of the casts' efforts to get the piece ready show. At the end they fall into a dejected heap. Silence.]

JANE: I feel cheap. Used.

JENNIFER: If Shakespeare had intended his plays to run for only five minutes then he'd have written them to last for only five minutes.

PETER: It cheapens us, Shakespeare, and the children.

JENNIFER: Why don't you say it, Jack? "I told you so."

CASH: There's no point. You know now I was right. I was bound to be right; you're serious about your work. If Gillian had experienced this, like you all, or if she could get INSIDE Shakespeare, she would sympathise with us.

JANE: But that's not possible.

CASH: Do you think the four of us can't come up with something?

PETER: You want us to conspire against her?

CASH: Not her! I want her to join us in a conspiracy against this government!

JANE: In *Romeo and Juliet* there are moments of silence that you can only experience in the theatre and we haven't been allowed to do this.

JENNIFER: What do you mean?

JANE: I mean... I think I mean that the plays themselves are conspiracies. Against authority. And it's in the silences that he works his mischief.

PETER: Mischief?

JANE: Yes. His potions; his spells. Puck's potions in *Midsummer Night's Dream*. Art is mischief! When you creatively use your mind you are engaging in mischief! What did Friar Lawrence say of the potion he gives to Juliet to make her appear dead? "Within the infant mind of this weak flower, poison hath residence, and medicine power..." "Within the infant mind" — he could be talking about these children. [*the audience*] And the poison is their own creative gifts. Their own imagination.

CASH: You're right, Jane. The imaginative force of the play is pushed on by love.

JANE: Love IS the politics of the heart.

CASH: Exactly.

PETER: So what?

CASH: Given what Jane's been saying about Puck and potions and the power of the imagination that they present, I'm thinking this. Supposing we have a party. In the woods. It's summer. Let's have a theme party. A *Mid-Summer Night's Dream* Party. We know the play!

PETER: What are you getting at? That we act the play?

CASH: No! How do we show how Shakespeare affects ordinary lives? By using our imagination in the way he did. We will invite Gillian to share in our conspiracy of imagination and it will clear up in her mind any confusion she may have about exactly what she should be.

JENNIFER: She'll only come if you invite her, Jack.

PETER: But for what?

CASH: God! Wake up, Peter! We can use masks, dress up, you name it. Just give her first hand contact with the play. Let her see for herself how absurd it is to trivialise such richness of imagination. Especially as in a *Midsummer Night's Dream* where illusion is piled high on illusion!

JANE &
JENNIFER: Let's do it!

PETER: I'm into a party, sure. I just think you're all being a bit optimistic! I can't see how it will work.

[*JANE hugs PETER. This seems excessive.*]

JANE: I knew you'd agree.

SCENE FOUR

[*Government Office. The GOVERNMENT OFFICER is writing a letter to GILLIAN.*]

G.O.: [*speaking as he writes*] Dear Ms Brutus. [*crosses out*] Dear Gillian, I am in a kind of turmoil. I have had to read *Romeo and Juliet* and suddenly your arguments seem so potent, I wonder what we are doing. The play is about how the young suffer at the hands of the old. It's a political play. The children are expected to act POLITICALLY but have no political rights. The older generation seems committed to condemning these poor children to miserable, difficult lives. [*pause*] We are always cutting away at our children's education, cutting away at their future! We are making political moves that effect their lives and expecting them to accommodate our changes AS THOUGH THEY WERE POLITICAL BEINGS! But we know they have no political rights, few rights at all. They must do as they are told. As they are instructed. [*pause*] I must also tell you that [*pause*] I LOVE, LOVE, LOVE YOU, DEEPLY, DEEPLY, DEEPLY!

[*He stops.*]

G.O.: What am I doing?!

[*He rips up the letter and throws it away. He picks up the phone.*]

G.O.: Oh, God! Answer-phone. [*pause*] Oh, hello. It's the Government Officer. Just to remind Ms Brutus that I'll be along to collect the *Romeo and Juliet* tape on... [*He looks at some papers.*] yes... Mid-Summer Night's Eve! Bye.

[*He puts the phone down.*]

Act Three

The Dance of Illusion

SCENE ONE

[*GILLIAN'S office. She is finishing-off getting ready. GILLIAN and CASH are dressed 'thematically'. They are both drinking copiously from a bottle of wine.*]

CASH: I'm glad you decided to come, Gillian. [*pause*] I believe that nature is an incubus invading every man — and woman's — sleep.

GILLIAN: I don't understand you.

CASH: Well, nature is very strong in Shakespeare. It counterbalances civilisation. In some cases it accounts for fate. The Ides of March in *Julius Caesar* are the answer to Caesar crossing the Rubicon. Civilised people make decisions like Caesar's but in the end there is a natural order.

GILLIAN: What's that got to do with tonight?

CASH: We're going into the woods! Back to nature! Outmanoeuvre the incubus before the night is full!
[*Pause.*]

GILLIAN: Who are you?

CASH: Well... for the sake of argument... Demetrius, I suppose.

GILLIAN: Who am I?

CASH: I'm not sure. Jane is Hermia, Peter is Lysander...

GILLIAN: Is that because Peter and Jane in real life are....

CASH: No, because, in fact, this IS real life. We're just

borrowing the names.

GILLIAN: Well, I don't want to be Helena!

CASH: Queen of the Faeries then, Titania. You know, the play, *A Midsummer Night's Dream*, is set in May, in the woods, and the title refers to the common custom of divining by midsummer dreams and flowers who one's lover was or whether one's lover was faithful.

GILLIAN: Why are you telling me this, Jack?

CASH: [*mischievously*] Because I wouldn't want you to go into the woods under any illusions!

GILLIAN: Well, if that's the case the real thing will do me! Come! Let us go where souls do couch on flowers!

[*Exeunt.*]

SCENE TWO

[*The woods. A moon. PETER is sitting. JANE is trying to get close to him. They are both drinking and waiting for something to happen.*]

PETER: The wood where Oberon was king is one where all travellers get lost.

JANE: LOVE is a wood where all travellers get lost!

PETER: Hmmm.

JANE: Wert thou as far as that vast shore wash'd with the farthest sea I should adventure by yonder blessèd moon, I vow, that tips with silver all these fruit-tree tops.

PETER: What?

JANE: [*sighs*] Nothing.

PETER: You know, Shakespeare knew a Welshman in

Stratford; WelshMEN I should say. He used a Welsh boy actor in *Henry VI* so it's not surprising that his fairies are more like Welsh fairies than any other kind.

[*JANE looks at PETER with something like disbelief.*]

PETER: A fact of some further interest in connection with his other fairy play, *The Merry Wives of Windsor*.

JANE;   [*jumping up*] This is supposed to be a party, not an English lesson! Where are the others?

PETER: I told you; they're probably lost.

JANE: I'm going to look.

[*JANE goes. After a moment, PETER goes.*]

SCENE THREE

[*CASH and GILLIAN come on.*]

GILLIAN: Goodness, I feel so tired! The wine must have gone straight to my head!

CASH: Let's rest here awhile, wait for the others.

GILLIAN: Hmmm! That's a good idea.

CASH: [*aside, looking around*] Where are they?

GILLIAN: What?

CASH: Nothing.

[*They lay down. CASH is on his back. GILLIAN is curled up next to him.*]

CASH: It's been another hard day.

[*They fall silent. PETER as PUCK comes on.*]

PETER: [*to Audience*]
                    When I feel a girl asleep

41

Underneath her frock I peep,
There to sport, and there I play,
then I bite her like a flea
And about I skip.

PETER: Here's some good mischief for me. Gillian is asleep and Jack Cash can't see me. If I just drop a little of this love juice on Gillian's eyes, then get rid of Jack, I will stand before her and she will fall in love with me because its power is that she will fall in love with he on whom first falls her gaze.

[*He drops potion on GILLIAN's eyes. He goes off.*]

PETER: [*Off, in a shouted whisper.*] Jack!

[*CASH looks up groggily. He sits up.*]

PETER: [*Off.*] Here! Come here!

[*CASH gets up, looks at GILLIAN and goes off. After a moment, PETER comes on. He takes a long swig from a bottle she's carrying. He stands over GILLIAN triumphantly.*]

PETER: Gillian!

[*GILLIAN wakes. She gasps.*]

GILLIAN: Peter!

[*She gets up. They embrace and kiss. JANE can be seen looking on glumly.*]

JANE: Only Oberon and Puck could be adults in this wood! The agèd to like children fly into each other's arms while these children [*the Audience*] would shrink from such ostentation.

GILLIAN: Oh, how I love you Peter and hope this love won't peter out!

SCENE FOUR

[*JANE, CASH*]

CASH: Jane! Lovers and madmen have such seething brains, the lunatic, the lover, and the poet, are of imagination all compact. The poet's eye, in a fine frenzy roll-ing, doth glance from heaven to earth, from earth to heaven; and as imagination bodies forth the forms of things unknown, the poet's pen turns them to shapes, and gives airy nothing a local habitation and a name.

JANE: [*distracted*] What are you talking about, Jack?

CASH: The poet, the lover, and the lunatic. Beneath the moon. You have made me a lunatic!

JANE: God, Jack! That's really cheap. You're pissed! That's what's making you mad.

[*CASH takes hold of JANE passionately.*]

CASH: No, Jane! Imagination. First there is the seed of an idea watered by the tears I have brought forth from your nightwatch eyes and then the bud and the flower.

JANE: Leave me alone, Jack! You smell like a brewery! Poetry is an illusion like madness and love-madness. The lover, the madman and the poet are all deluded; what they see is not there and what they say is false. YOU would have said that yesterday!

CASH: But I wasn't brought into the verse, then. Into the play. I didn't know the power of the song! Kiss me!

[*JANE sighs.*]

JANE: All right, Jack. But just a little one. And I want something in return.

CASH: Anything!

[*They kiss.*]

JANE: Where's Jennifer?

CASH: [*breathlessly*] I... I don't know.

JANE: [*holding him off*] Find her, Jack. If you want anything more to do with me tonight.

CASH: But why?

JANE: Just do it. Love?

CASH: Wait? Wait for me.

[*CASH hurries off.*]

JANE: I'm bitten! Smitten. The little green mosquito has
given me love's worst malaria: jealousy. Peter
loves Gillian! How could I have not seen it? They
will be marrying here in the wood before the
moon has fallen into a dead man's arms.

SCENE FIVE

[*JANE and JENNIFER.*]

JANE: Jennifer, I have seen Peter.

JENNIFER: Where? Tell me!

JANE: He's with GILLIAN.

JENNIFER: Oh, no! Then swallows have built in Peter's sails
their nests!

JANE: But I think it's a mistake. Peter is probably drunk.
He must think he's with you! Let us go, you and I,
and change the love in his arms for the love of his
mind.

JENNIFER: But who is that?

JANE: You!

JENNIFER: Me?

JANE: Of course! But you must let him continue believing he is with Gillian.

JENNIFER: But you said he must be thinking he's with me.

JANE: Yes, that's what I say. But I can't read his mind. Maybe he's been duped, tricked into believing that who he really wants is Gillian, but when he comes to his senses brought on by the touch of your trembling body then he will be grateful to you for showing him that it's you he loves, not her! So grateful will he be that love will be enhanced. Better that than in shock of a confused discovery his natural joy should be twisted by starry circumstances into resentment!

JENNIFER: Oh.

JANE: Go on then!

JENNIFER: But where are they?

JANE: Follow that path.

           [*JENNIFER goes.*]

JANE: This is my plan: once Jennifer has replaced Gillian in the arms of MY love, then I will tell Peter that the great riches of his affection are being spent on the wrong woman! Then, in the terrible confusion of his account, with his bank balance in the red, I will offer the deposit of my heart which he will accept!

           [*She runs off.*]

SCENE SIX

[*PETER and GILLIAN are laying on their backs.*]

45

GILLIAN: I feel so tired!

PETER: And me.

GILLIAN: Let me climb into your eyes and sleep!

[*They roll over and face each other. They close their eyes. JANE as PUCK appears.*]

JANE: One drop of this confusing potion on their eyes and Gillian will walk as in her sleep while Peter on waking will think that in his arms is the Gillian twin not the Jennifer! Jennifer will say she's Gillian but I will reveal she is Jennifer!

[*She drops potion. GILLIAN gets up asleep and walks off. JANE kneels down and almost kisses PETER but withdraws before she does. JANE jumps up as JENNIFER comes on and, directed by JANE, lays down beside PETER. JANE tickles PETER'S nose. As he wakes she runs off though she can be seen looking on. PETER wakes.*]

PETER: Spread girl thy rosy cheeks, tinted with pink of Tyrian vermilion, give lips, coral lips; give gentle kisses like a dove, part of the sap of the living soul.

JENNIFER: Ooooo!

[*She kisses PETER. JANE huffs and goes.*]

SCENE SEVEN

[*CASH is wandering disconsolately.*]

CASH: Come Philostrate! Stir up this valley's girl to merriment! Awake in her the pert and nimble spirit of mirth. [*He sits.*] Oh, I am so unhappy! So... unconsolidated.

[*The GOVERNMENT OFFICER comes on. He is carrying a bunch of flowers.*]

G.O.: Ah! You there! I am looking for the members of the Shakespeare Factory.

CASH: [*angrily*] Do you know that there are many who believe that not Shakespeare but Francis Bacon wrote Shakespeare's plays? If they were right would you then ask for members of the Bacon Factory?

G.O.: [*confused*] I don't understand!...

CASH: It could put us out of business! Invalidate everything! How can you teach children the plays of Shakespeare when they are the plays of Francis Bacon? It is a lesson in forgery! Deceit! The worst kind of illusion. Illusion without the saving grace of playfulness. Illusion designed to CHEAT!

[*CASH takes hold of the GOVERNMENT OFFICER.*]

G.O.: Unhand me, man!

CASH: Francis Bacon died watching the halting effect of snow on the decaying of a dead chicken. That is all you need to know about the relationship of mortality to time.

[*Silence.*]

G.O.: [*nervously*] I'm looking, ac...ac...actually, for Gillian Brutus.

CASH: Why?

G.O.: I'm... I'm from the government.

CASH: Government? What government?

G.O.: The... the one... the one in Westminster.

CASH: You mean... You mean... the BRITISH government?

G.O.: Yes.

[*CASH lets out a terrible cry and savagely manhandles the GOVERNMENT OFFICER. He is about to hit*] *him then stops.*]

CASH: [*to Audience*] Fool me! This is the Government Official come to collect the video. I had forgotten! And now here he is as if by magic and I have an idea! A scent of mischief has assailed my some-time virgin nose!

[*CASH unhandles GOVERNMENT OFFICER. He brushes him down.*]

CASH: My sincere apologies. I recognise you now.

[*CASH produces a bottle.*]

CASH: Have a drink.

G.O.: Oh, well....

[*GOVERNMENT OFFICER takes bottle and drinks tentatively.*]

CASH: Take a BIG drink!

G.O.: But I'm... I'm not really a drinker.

CASH: [*expansively*] Hey man! Who is really anything?

[*GOVERNMENT OFFICER drinks deep. GILLIAN comes on looking confused.*]

CASH: Jennifer!

[*He takes her aside so that GOVERNMENT OFFI-CER can't hear.*]

CASH: Jennifer! Have you seen Gillian?

[*He indicates GOVERNMENT OFFICER.*]

JENNIFER: Jack, it's me! I'm Gillian!

CASH: You?

GILLIAN: Of course! Oh, Jack! I love you!

[*She leaps at CASH and kisses him. CASH struggles and frees himself. He lets out a loud ass's noise.*]

GILLIAN: Jack! What is it? You sound like a donkey!

CASH: It's my bottom! I mean, I am Bottom!

[*He lets out more ass noises and runs off, pursued by GILLIAN. JANE comes on. She looks off after GILLIAN and CASH.*]

JANE: Why is Gillian chasing Jack? What is she? Is this what power does that she thinks she has in her important fingers the rhythm of every man's heart? She is not satisfied with flower-bedding my latest love, she also wants my last!

[*She sees the GOVERNMENT OFFICER.*]

JANE: Who is this? A drunken, suited sot? [*to GOVERNMENT OFFICER*] Who are you?

G.O.: I am the officer of the government.

JANE: He is mad! Caught up in the lunatic twists of a tale of love!

G.O.: I am a gent of governing spurned.

JANE: Spurned? Who hath spurned you?

G.O.: Ms Gillyfun Brutearse.

JANE: I beg your pardonechtomy! [*to Audience*] He's come for Gillian. This could be one twin twisted out of her purpose to leave the other legless! [*to GOVERNMENT OFFICER*] Let me help you up. [*She points him the way CASH and GILLIAN went.*] Follow that path and you will, before the moon is another minute old, find your brutal woman incumbent upon a Shop Steward who will direct you, I dare say, to her affection!

[*She pushes GOVERNMENT OFFICER OFF.*]

JANE: What a night!
    I will be treble-sinew'd, hearted, breath'd,
And fight maliciously. For when mine hours
Were nice and lucky, men did ransom lives

Of me for jests; but now I'll set my teeth,
And send to darkness all that stop me.
Anthony and Cleopatra!
[*She rushes off.*]

SCENE EIGHT

[*PETER and JENNIFER. They kiss, cuddle and giggle.*]

PETER: Let's grant it is not amiss to tumble on the bed of Ptolemy!

BOTH: Ha, ha, ha!

[*They drink.*]

JENNIFER: Let us have one other gaudy night!

BOTH: Ha, ha, ha!

PETER: I feel I have tasted enough fullness of lips to fill all of time!

JENNIFER: And I feel I have tasted of full time and really need a bit extra!

PETER: [*hugging JENNIFER*] I never thought! I never thought!

JENNIFER: What?

PETER: That I would be spending the night with you!

[*JANE rushes on.*]

JANE: You're not.

PETER: What?

JANE: You're not spending the evening with her — I mean who you think she is. You're not spending your evening with Gillian. It's Jennifer. You're confused. You can't think straight.

JENNIFER: She's lying, Peter!

JANE: Who ever loved that loved not at first sight?

PETER: But I did love at first sight! From the moment I first saw Gillian!

JANE: But that is Jennifer.

[*Pause while PETER thinks. He holds JENNIFER'S face.*]

PETER: That face is the face I first fell in love with. Everything about it: the shape of the eyes, how it conveys in them innocence in sadness; the playful harmless nose that unobtrusively carries its obtrusiveness, to the mouth; that wonderful mouth that, pursed, blew full sail the Trojan fleet as Paris left Greece with his stolen bride.

JANE: But it is only apparently so. It's an illusion! Jennifer is the illusion of Gillian.

[*PETER hesitates.*]

PETER: Well... well... I have tasted more secret delights which cause me not to care!

JANE: Care about what?

PETER: Care whether you were right! Because if you WERE right, in this case, in this wild wood, what is only apparently so is really so. If she were Jennifer she has, nevertheless, the face I first pursued in dreams and now in this night that dream has become flesh and I have discovered our humanity.

JANE: I will bring you Gillian and then we'll see how careless you are. It's just drink talking.

[*She rushes off.*]

PETER: I don't care! I don't care! Ha, ha, ha!

JENNIFER: 'Twas I; but 'tis not I, I do not shame

To tell you what I was, since my conversion
So sweetly tastes, being the thing I am.

PETER: But you were what you are. And you ARE here!
[*He embraces her. They kiss.*]

SCENE NINE

[*CASH is wandering aimlessly, a little drunk. JANE enters. They bump into each other.*]

CASH: [*Falling to his knees.*] Oh, Jane, Jane! Jane! Give me leave to speak my mind, and I will through and through cleanse the foul body of th'infected world!

JANE: What do you mean? What are you talking about?

CASH: This night! This world of the woods where what we dream and imagine seems more powerful than what is! Where our plotting supplants the plots we're born with. You were born to love me.

[*He holds onto JANE'S legs.*]

JANE: Oh, Jack! I don't know. I am so confused. The power of the play has turned my head from mere playing. I feel my life has changed.

CASH: Oh, when I sat in Babylon, Jane, I dreamed the rivers of the desert froze.

JANE: Oh, sweet Jack, his torment has made him babble on.

CASH: Oh, come with me and be my love and we will all the pleasures prove!

[*The GOVERNMENT OFFICER comes on drunk. He sits helplessly on a tuft. They look at him in silence for a moment.*]

G.O.: You Banbury cheese!

Ay, it is no matter,
How now, Mephistopheles!
Ay, it is no matter.
Slice, I say! Pauca, pauca! Slice! That's my humour.

CASH: He's gone!

JANE: He's mad!

CASH: I have an idea! Jane, stay, entertain him and I'll be back.

[*He rushes off.*]

G.O.: [*to JANE*] I am bowl'd to death with turnips.

JANE: I know, I know. It's common enough. You shouldn't feel guilty.

G.O.: I will knock his urinals about his knave's costard when I have goot opportunities for the ork.

JANE: I didn't think life could be so profound. [*aside*] Hurry, Jack! I'm seeing the fall of the British Empire at my feet!

G.O.: By gar, he shall not have a stone to throw at his dog. Piss my tallow!

JANE: Do you need the toilet?

G.O.: Gor-unmeant gusset. By gar, de herring is no dead so as I vill kill him!

[*He suddenly jumps up and falls in a heap.*]

JANE: Oh, no!

[*She puts an ear to his heart to see if he's still alive. She gasps with relief. She sits down and puts her head between her legs. CASH as PUCK comes on.*]

CASH: Two ticks and I'll have his whole life changed!

[*He props GOVERNMENT OFFICER up in sitting position.*]

CASH: And a couple of drops of this love juice in each eye and when he wakes he will fall so deeply in love with whomsoever he sees!

[*He drops love juice in GOVERNMENT OFFICER'S eyes. He goes off. He returns with an ass's head. He puts head on GOVERNMENT OFFICER. He replaces flowers in G.O.'S arms. He goes, making donkey noises. This causes JANE to look up. She sees ass's head and screams and runs off. After a moment, a half-drunk GILLIAN comes on being gently guided by CASH as PUCK. She sees the GOVERNMENT OFFICER with ass's head.*]

GILLIAN: Am I to be ridden by a Welsh goat too? No! No! It's Jack! My Jack in an ass's head! Oh, my Jack!
　　Come sit down on this flow'ry bed,
　　While I thy amiable cheeks do coy,
　　And stick musk-roses [*uses his flowers*]
　　　　in thy sleek smooth head,
　　and kiss thy fair large ears, my gentle joy.

[*She sits next to GOVERNMENT OFFICER and soon falls asleep with an arm around him.*]

CASH: [*as PUCK*] Now for the coup de theatre! The cream on the pudding of my plotting! Two drops on the eyes of Gillian and when she wakes she will love this ass like no other ass was ever loved!

[*He drops love juice.*]

SCENE TEN

[*JANE comes on. She stops for a moment.*]

JANE: I am done for by my own plotting! I made one more appeal to Peter and all he said was thank you! He said if I hadn't showed him he would never have realised how much he loves Jennifer!

[*She suddenly stamps her feet in a tantrum. CASH comes on.*]

CASH: [*timidly*] Jane?

JANE: Oh, Jack! Jack! I'm so tired!

[*She falls into CASH'S arms.*]

CASH: I cannot by the progress of the stars guess how near to day we are but I do believe the stars have a little last mischief to play. Come with me.

SCENE ELEVEN

[*GILLIAN and GOVERNMENT OFFICER in ass's head. CASH and JANE are looking on.*]

JANE: We should turn him off, like the empty ass, to shake his ears and graze in commons.

CASH: No! Watch! We may yet be revenged even with the sword that would kill us.

[*GOVERNMENT OFFICER wakes.*]

G.O.: Oh, my head is heavy! And it is caged about by a dark mean inner skin like I had woken up inside a grape! But who is this [*GILLIAN*] Oh, I am in deepest love! What has happened tonight? I feel as if I walked into a world that was in some other's mind made and it's changed my own life forever! [*He holds GILLIAN.*] But I can't reach her lips with mine! What has happened? [*He feels his face. He cries out.*] Cancer! My nose is tumoured and become a barn upon my face!

[*GILLIAN wakes.*]

GILLIAN: Oh, my ass! My sweet ass! How I love your great horse's cheeks like a big man's bum!

[*CASH and JANE laugh. GOVERNMENT OFFICER*

takes off ass's head. He looks at it in amazement.]

G.O.: An ass's head!

GILLIAN: You! I am so... so moved! My life is changed as though last night I lived a dream! But why are you here! The video! You've come to collect the video! I'd forgotten!

G.O.: No, I came to bring you these.

[*He gives her flowers. They embrace. CASH and JANE come on.*]

CASH: You lived last night inside Shakespeare's dream, his play, in the great sweep of his imagination.

GILLIAN: Then you were right! [*to GOVERNMENT OFFICER*] And you were wrong.

G.O.: But I came to tell you!...

GILLIAN: What?

G.O.: That I was wrong. We need to educate children in Shakespeare not just dish him out as a sop to tradition.

GILLIAN: So you'll help us?

JANE: Our spirit, the people's spirit, raging for
                        revenge,
With Até by our side come hot from hell,
Shall in these confines with a sovereign voice
Cry 'Havoc!' and let slip the dogs of war,
That this foul deed — of government cuts — shall smell above the earth
With carrion men, groaning for burial.

CASH: [*to GOVERNMENT OFFICER*] Will you help us?

[*Pause.*]

G.O.: Far from that country Pindarus shall run, where never Roman shall take note of him.

GILLIAN: NO! Where every Englishman will take note! Will you help us? [*pause*]

G.O.:   Yes!

            [*They cheer. Both couples hug and kiss.*]

G.O.:   We are ordinary people and we have been deeply
            affected.

GILLIAN: Where is Jennifer? Peter?

CASH: Jennifer has swallowed fire and died!

            [*They laugh.*]

JANE: She is buried in Peter's sighs!

            [*They laugh.*]

EPILOGUE

Our revels are now ended. These our actors
it may be said, were all spirits, and
are melted into air, into thin air;
and, like the baseless fabric of this vision,
all which it inherit, shall dissolve,
and, like this insubstantial pageant faded,
leave not a rack behind. We are such stuff
as dreams are made on; and our little life
is rounded with a sleep, BUT we are the sleepers
and we are the dreams and though we may not
know the schemes of gods and such who play
with molecules like errant boys with worms,
we cannot leave it to those whose power
is no less an illusion than our brave
struggling to tell us how our minds may
weave their stories. We are all Shakespeare's
children. Remember, first to possess his books
before others possess us by the taking of ours.

[*Exeunt.*]

Moon River: The Deal

Notes to the Original Production

Moon River: The Deal was commissioned by Spectacle Theatre with support from the Arts Council of Wales. This play was first performed on February 16th, 1993 at Pont Rhondda Primary, Rhondda Fawr.

Directed by	Steve Davis
Designed by	Janis Hart
Musical Direction	Paula Gardiner

Cast

Bryn	D.R. Lyn
Colin	Alan Grice
Miss	Caroline Bunce
Charley	Miranda Ballin
Mr Bennet-Jones	Alan Grice
Mrs Bennet-Jones	Caroline Bunce
Bryn's Mum	Caroline Bunce
Bryn's Dad	Alan Grice

Act One
SCENE ONE

[*A classroom. BRYN and COLIN POPE are kneeling on the floor. Before them they each have a jam-jar, a piece of blotting paper and a bean.*]

BRYN: How do we do it?

COLIN: She'll tell us in a minute.

BRYN: Well you have to put the bean on the blotting paper, that's obvious. [*He does this.*] You do it. [*COLIN does it.*] I think it needs to be wet.

[*BRYN dribbles onto his bean.*]

COLIN: Oh, no! You pig! You wait until Miss sees that!

BRYN: I'll put the glass over it. [*He does.*] See? Like a greenhouse. Now we need some sun. You can bless it with the sun. You're the Pope! Ha, ha, ha!

COLIN: Shurrup! You know I hate that!

BRYN: But it's your name!

COLIN: I know that! I knows what my name is!

BRYN: Pope, Pope, Colin Pope, Pope, Pope, Colin Pope!

COLIN: Shurrup!

[*Silence.*]

BRYN: What if you put a 'the' in there?

COLIN: Where?

BRYN: In your name.

            [*Pause.*]

COLIN: THE Colin Pope? That makes me sound, that makes me sound BIG.

BRYN: No! Colin THE Pope!

COLIN: Colin THE Pope? The Pope the thing?

BRYN: The vicar.

COLIN: I told you, don't say that!

BRYN: I was only joking, it's a free world.

COLIN: What's a free world?

BRYN: Haven't you heard people say that? My dad always says it.

COLIN: What do you mean? He gets things for nothing?

BRYN: 'Course not.

COLIN: But that's free.

BRYN: Not that!!

COLIN: Well, if it's not that it's stupid.

BRYN: It's not stupid, I'll show you.

COLIN: How?

BRYN: Swop beans.

COLIN: I like my bean!

BRYN: I like my bean too! It's just as good as your bean!

COLIN: Well, even if we swapped this would still be mine.

BRYN: Only because it's in front of you.

COLIN: It would still be mine even if you put your name on it, I'll prove it! Put your name on it.

BRYN: There's no need to go so far. It'll kill the bean.

COLIN: Not the bean! The blotting paper. [*silence*] Do it or I'll punch your face in!

BRYN: If that's what you want.

[*BRYN writes his name on COLIN'S blotting paper.*]

COLIN: Miss, Miss, Miss! Brynley Morgan wrote on my blotting paper! Miss, Miss, he's ruined my bean. Miss!

[*MISS comes on.*]

MISS: Well, Brynley, did you? Did you?

BRYN: No, Miss. No.

MISS: You did! You did it! I know you!

BRYN: Miss, Colin's lying, Miss!

COLIN: No! I'm not, Miss! I'm not, Miss, honest!

MISS: I know, I know. Let me see. Let me see it, Colin. Oh, yes, I can see. You DID do it, didn't you, Brynley Morgan? You did it, I can see you did it. It's all over you. It's all over your face.

BRYN: No, Miss. Miss it wasn't me!

MISS: Is your name Brynley Morgan?

BRYN: Yes, Miss.

MISS: Yes, Miss. And would Colin put your name on his bean?

BRYN: It's not on his bean, Miss! That's what I said! I said if you write on the bean, it'll die!

MISS: On the blotting paper! You know what I'm talking about! Would Colin put your name on his blotting paper? Would he? Well, would he?

BRYN: But he told me, Miss! He told me!

MISS: TOLD you? TOLD you? Are you telling me that he TOLD you to put your name on his bean, blotting paper, and that then he's telling ME that you put your name on his bean as if he didn't want it! The bean?

BRYN: Yes, Miss! He told me!

MISS: Well, Brynley Morgan, I don't believe you. And that's a terrible thing for me to say that I don't believe one of the children but I've got no choice because it's true and that makes me feel terrible.

BRYN: So believe me, Miss, then you won't.

MISS: Won't what?

BRYN: Feel terrible!

MISS: Right! That's it! I'll see your father and we'll see what he says about a son who's a cheeky liar. A liar! A downright liar!

BRYN: Miss! Miss! No, don't tell Dad, Miss! He'll, he'll, he'll, he'll, he'll...

[*Lights down.*]

SCENE TWO

[*The sound of a river. Charlotte is fishing. She's known as CHARLEY. She's dressed as a boy. She's humming 'Moon River'. Suddenly she stops, listens, gets up and picks up her knife and stands defensively.*]

CHARLEY: Who is it? Who's there?

[*BRYN comes on.*]

CHARLEY: A kid! [*She sits, putting the knife down.*] You spying on me? Who sent you?

BRYN: N-n-n-no one.

CHARLEY: Then why you here?

MOON RIVER: THE DEAL

BRYN: I've run away.

CHARLEY: You've run away?

BRYN: Yeah.

CHARLEY: Why?

BRYN: Because teacher was going to tell my Dad about me.

CHARLEY: About you, what?

BRYN: About when we were growing beans on blotting paper.

CHARLEY: The teacher was going to tell your father that you were growing beans? What is he, a nut?

BRYN: No, a woman.

CHARLEY: O.K., so what did you do? Grow a homicidal bean?

BRYN: No. I wrote on Colin Pope's blotting paper.

CHARLEY: I hate that!

BRYN: W-w-why?

CHARLEY: It's the worst thing you could do!

BRYN: Why?

CHARLEY: Because you know what blotting paper does?

BRYN: It — um — grows beans.

CHARLEY: No, no dummy! It soaks up stuff.

BRYN: I don't get it.

CHARLEY: It's like you. You're like a piece of blotting paper. As you grow up you soak things up. It's called learning how to live. How would you like to be written on? FORCED to soak things up? They wanted to write all over me!

BRYN: [*tearfully*] But he asked me to do it!

CHARLEY: Who did?

BRYN: Colin Pope!

CHARLEY: You mean he asked you to write on his blotting paper then he shopped you for doing it?

BRYN: No.

CHARLEY: What?

BRYN: He told on me.

CHARLEY: That's what I said! He shopped you. That's what it means. What're you? Some kind of Neanderthal Man?

BRYN: What's that?

CHARLEY: It doesn't matter, he turned you in and that's tragic. Sounds like it's a kind of love/hate thing he's got for you. I've seen that kind of thing before.

BRYN: LOVE!

CHARLEY: Not snogging love. Love like... what you feel for your dog.

BRYN: I haven't got a dog.

CHARLEY: Well, what you would feel for your dog if you had a dog! [*pause*] It's a tragic thing.

BRYN: What?

CHARLEY: That we have to go through life without a dog. Think what we could learn.

BRYN: What?

CHARLEY: Well, you could have learned about how Colin Pope loved you! [*pause*] Want to lay low with me for a while?

BRYN: Where?

CHARLEY: Here, I got a hide-out.

MOON RIVER: THE DEAL

BRYN: Here? You live here? By the river?

CHARLEY: Sure.

BRYN: O.K.

CHARLEY: Just behave yourself.

           [*BRYN settles down.*]

BRYN: What's your name?

CHARLEY: Charley.

BRYN: How long have you lived here?

CHARLEY: A day. I was in the city for a while, Cardiff. I
           didn't like it.

BRYN: You've run away from Cardiff?

CHARLEY: No! From here. I lived further down the valley. I
           ran away from there. Down to the city.

BRYN: Why?

CHARLEY: I'm an orphan.

BRYN: What happened to your Mum and Dad?

CHARLEY: Got killed when I was a kid. My Gran brought me
           up. But she used to get ill. So I'd get fostered out.
           You know what that is?

BRYN: No.

CHARLEY: You go to people who ACT like your parents for a
           night then you go back home. They were called
           [*posh accent*] The Bennett-Joneses. It was OK as
           long as I could go home. But then Gran died.
           [*pause*] So they wanted me to be their kid full-
           time. Adopted.

BRYN: What's wrong with that?

CHARLEY: Hey don't patronise me, kid! It's tragic! The
           trouble with people like [*posh*] the Bennett-Joneses
           is they want you to be like them. They think that

being like them is the right thing. But I think that being like me is the right thing and I want to be like me! They don't even know what being like them is!

BRYN: I don't get that.

CHARLEY: Listen. You got any imagination?

BRYN: Yeah.

CHARLEY: Well, shut your eyes and I'll show them to you.

BRYN: Who?

CHARLEY: The Bennett-Joneses!

BRYN: Oh! O.K.

CHARLEY: Shut?

BRYN: Yeah.

CHARLEY: I was staying with them one night. I could hear them talking. They were talking about me. So I · went down to listen.

[MR & MRS BENNETT-JONES come on. They sit either side of a table.]

MRS. B.J.: The child needs love and the safety of a home.

MR. B.J.: But Mair, such a child will grow up to be lazy and selfish. The child needs discipline. Her life must be ordered. She must be told what to do; what to think.

MRS. B.J.: But, John! Such a child will grow up to be afraid of you. Afraid of me! I want a child to hold and care for!

MR. B.J.: You want a child just to cuddle! You want a doll. I want a child with a place in society who can hold her head up high.

MRS. B.J.: You want a child who can hold YOUR head up high! But I want a child who is sweet and needs me.

MR. B.J.: You want a child who IS a sweet that you need! I want a child who will follow without question the rules of society.

MRS. B.J.: You want a child who won't walk on the grass because you're afraid she might bring mud into the house! But I want a child who will fill the house with her playing; with her smile!

MR. B.J.: But you want a child who's a poodle! I want a child who's a guard dog! Someone who can defend MY beliefs; MY society!

MRS. B.J.: Well, I DON'T want a child who's a doberman! I don't want a child who's a policeman. I'd rather a child in need!

MR. B.J.: The trouble with you, Mair, is that you don't know what you want a child for!

[*MRS BENNETT-JONES cries out in frustration and rushes off.*]

MR. B.J.: Well, I don't think a tantrum helps! [*pause*] Mair!

[*MR BENNETT-JONES runs off after her.*]

CHARLEY: Did you see them?

BRYN: Yeah!

CHARLEY: The imagination is a powerful thing.

BRYN: Yeah!

CHARLEY: That's what he said: "What you want a child FOR"! Like it was one of those things for peeling potatoes! And TANTRUMS! [*suddenly*] Hey! Does anybody know you run away?

BRYN: Only Colin.

CHARLEY: Colin?

BRYN: Yeah. It was his idea. He said if I went home my Dad'd kill me. Anyway, why? What's the matter?

CHARLEY: Because if they don't know you've run away, your parents'll phone the police and they'll have a search party out for you!

BRYN: Well, what about you?

CHARLEY: What about me?

BRYN: No one's searching for you. ˙

CHARLEY: Hey! I am long lost. Written off. Once they knew I'd gone to the city.

BRYN: Written off?

CHARLEY: Yeah. Missing person. Haven't you seen it on TV? There's thousands of kids missing in this country. They're never found 'cos they're written off. People won't say it because they think they're dead. And that's the trick. If you're going to stay out any length of time you gotta become a missing person.

BRYN: What's the trick?

CHARLEY: If they think you're a missing person — meaning you're dead — they won't talk about it. So you get written off.

BRYN: So how do you become a missing person?

CHARLEY: By staying out a long time.

BRYN: But you said to stay out you've got to become a missing person!

CHARLEY: That's life, kid! And also, you got to let them think you've gone to the city.

BRYN: How do we do that?

CHARLEY: I'm working on it.

[*Silence. CHARLEY picks up fishing gear. BRYN picks up book.*]

BRYN: Do you like reading books?

CHARLEY: This is more than a book, kid. It's a way of life.

BRYN: What do you mean?

CHARLEY: It shows you how important kids are.

BRYN: [*sadly*] I don't think they are, not according to teachers and parents.

CHARLEY: What do they know? *Huckleberry Finn* made America.

BRYN: Who?

CHARLEY: *Huckleberry Finn*, the book. I'll read some. Listen to this. It's about Tom Sawyer's gang.

BRYN: I thought you said it was Huckleberry Finn.

CHARLEY: Just listen. "...Tom made everybody swear to keep the secret, and then he showed them a hole in the hill, right in the thickest part of the bushes. Then we lit the candles and crawled in on our hands and knees. We went about two hundred yards, and then the cave opened up. Tom poked about amongst the passages and pretty soon ducked under a wall where you wouldn't a noticed that there was a hole. We went along a narrow place and got into a kind of room, all damp and sweaty and cold, and there we stopped."

That's like my place! My hideout.

[*reading*] "Tom says: 'Now we'll start this band of robbers and call it Tom Sawyer's Gang. Everybody that wants to join has got to take the oath, and write his name in blood. Everybody was willing. So Tom got out a sheet of paper that he had wrote the oath on, and read it. It swore every boy to stick to the band, and never tell any of the secrets; and if anybody done anything to any boy in the band, whichever boy was ordered to kill that person and his family must do it, and he musn't eat and he musn't sleep till he had killed

71

them and hacked a cross on their breasts, which was the sign of the band. And nobody that didn't belong to the band could use that mark, and if he did he must be sued; and if he done it again he must be killed. And if anybody that belonged to the band told the secrets, he must have his throat cut, and then have his carcass burnt up and the ashes scattered all around, and his name blotted off of the list with blood and never mentioned again by the gang, but have a curse put on it and be forgot, for ever."

BRYN: That's disgusting. You can't do that. You can't kill people.

CHARLEY: Listen, "Everybody said it was a real beautiful oath and asked Tom if he got it out of his own head. He said, some of it, but the rest was out of pirate books and robber books and every gang that was high-toned had it." Gerritt?

BRYN: Get what?

CHARLEY: It's out of a book.

BRYN: It's scary.

CHARLEY: "Some thought it would be good to kill the *families* of boys that told the secrets. Tom said it was a good idea, so he took a pencil and wrote in it. Then Ben Rogers says: 'Here's Huck Finn, he hain't got no family — what you going to do 'bout him?'"

[*CHARLEY suddenly closes book.*]

BRYN: What's the matter?

CHARLEY: [*angry*] Nothing. It's nothing, O.K.? What's it got to do with you?

BRYN: Sorry.

[*CHARLEY picks up fishing gear.*]

CHARLEY: It's O.K. Come on. Time to get home.

BRYN: Home?

CHARLEY: The hideaway.

BRYN: Oh, yeah. [*pause*] You haven't caught any fish!

CHARLEY: No. But just imagine I've caught a big, fat salmon and we can roast it on a barbecue all juicy and tasty.

BRYN: So have we got anything to eat?

CHARLEY: Yeah. I've got a tin of pilchards.

[*They go. Lights down.*]

SCENE THREE

[*BRYN'S home. BRYN'S MUM is shouting upwards as though up the stairs.*]

MUM: [*tearfully*] You say that the police have said that they won't do anything, CAN'T do anything because Bryn's only run away. But what if he ran away into someone who might hurt him? I don't know how to deal with this, Derek! I wasn't taught how to! If I could lay my hands on him I'd knock him into the middle of next week! A kid can run away to Cardiff or maybe even London and never be seen again as if he was dead and no one will do anything because they KNOW he's run away. But if they only THINK he's been taken then they'll look for him with search parties and tracker dogs and TV cameras. And maybe even YOU! You say you can't do anything about it; that NO one can do anything about it! I can't even THINK about it because I wasn't taught how to deal with something like this, DEREK! If we can't do anything about our runaway son then we don't even belong in our own valley let alone the world!

[*Lights down.*]

SCENE FOUR

[*COLIN comes on. He stands alone looking off-stage.*]

COLIN: Peeled? Yes, sir! [*Pause*] Yes, sir! [*Pause*] Yes, sir! [*Pause*] Yes, sir! [*Pause*] Yes, sir! John Wayne!

[*COLIN turns to audience. He wears a sheriff's badge.*]

COLIN: PC Williams said "Colin Pope, I am making you my deputy". He said: "I want you to keep your eyes, ears and NOSE peeled." I said: "Peeled!" He said "Yes, son". I said: "Yes, sir!" He said: "We have to find this boy and because he's your friend — he is your friend, isn't he?" I said: "Yes, sir!" "Well" he said, "because he's your friend, you'll want more than anyone else to find him, isn't that so?" and I said: "Yes, sir!" And he said: "So, I'm making you my deputy. You understand?" And I said: "Yes, sir!" He said: "As in cowboy films which you have seen, I dare say?" And I said: "Yes, sir! John Wayne!"

[*COLIN goes. MRS BENNET-JONES comes on.*]

MRS B.J.: Yes, I'm bitter. Charley was my last chance. To have a child. Since she's gone I still make her bed every day. Every day. From the beginning. And in the act of remaking it I'm able to remember fully my Charley. I've made this room Charley's little world. My husband and I papered it with beautiful paper. Just what we thought she'd like. Everything. And Charley's gone! They said it's not uncommon these days! But we had the world to give her!

[*She cries. She lays on the bed.*]

74

MRS B.J.:   [*still laying down*] I don't understand. There are rules. If children stick to the rules we can ALL be happy. I could have made Charley like me. Why shouldn't she want what I've got? We allow children to have too many ideas! It must be the schools. I would send Charley to a public school where because I PAY, I would have the authority to say what I want her education to be. The school should teach children to recite tables, recite poems, teach them to RECITE and they will not run away! They will be happy with what they've got. Especially when it's as much as I can give.

[*BRYN'S DAD comes on. He shouts upwards as his wife did before.*]

DAD: Betty! [*pause*] Stop crying! Bryn's alright, I can feel it, I'd know it if he wasn't, I'd feel it. They'd 'ave found him if he was dead. He's mitched off, that's all. I feel angry! He should have had a belt now and again. But you can't do that anymore. If the teachers could belt them they'd be too scared to mitch off. That's all it is, Betty! A big mitch! Maybe the biggest mitch in the history of the valleys. Six days! I bet he's gone to Cardiff. They're all doing it now. But you wait when it gets cold. It'll be a different story. It's not like in our day. The conductor on the bus would have said: "Hey you, kid, where you going? Why aren't you in school?" But now they've got no conductors! They haven't even got mitching officers! He's probably right this very minute sitting in some burger bar, Burger King, Wimpy, McDonald's, you name it, stuffing his face full of greasy bits of beef!

[*He cries out and goes off. Lights down.*]

SCENE FIVE

[*Sound of river. CHARLEY is fishing. BRYN throws a stone.*]

CHARLEY: Hey! Have you gone crazy? You'll frighten the fish away!

BRYN: If there was any fish in there they'd be like burned sticks! I'm hungry, Charley! One pilchard a day isn't enough. And you never catch anything. There's no fish in there!

CHARLEY: So? Supposing there ISN'T any fish? I'm making a poem!

BRYN: What you mean? A rhyme?

CHARLEY: No!

BRYN: Well, teacher said that's what a poem means. It's a rhyme.

CHARLEY: That's stupid! A poem means what it says!

BRYN: So what's a poem?

CHARLEY: A poem?

BRYN: Yeah.

CHARLEY: It's a way of saying something.

BRYN: That's what I said! Like a rhyme.

CHARLEY: No! It's got to be a way of saying something that's different from the way you'd say something if you were just saying something normal.

BRYN: What like... [*pause*] I hate teachers.

CHARLEY: What!

BRYN: That's saying something normal.

CHARLEY: Not like that! Look. See that log over there?

BRYN: Yeah.

CHARLEY: You can look at it and say it's a log. But I can look at it and say it's a bridge. Not only that but it's a golden bridge shining in the sun.

BRYN: I don't gerrit.

CHARLEY: You don't get what?

BRYN: I don't get what's the point of saying a log is a bridge. Especially when it's not going anywhere.

CHARLEY: It's in my mind, my 'ead dummy! It's what I'm saying. So it's my bridge. And it's going somewhere. It's going over the Moon River.

BRYN: Moon River?

CHARLEY: Yeah.

BRYN: Is there any such place?

CHARLEY: 'Course there is.

BRYN: Well, where? Where is it?

CHARLEY: In my 'ead! I told you! My 'magination.

BRYN: [angry] But what's the point?!

CHARLEY: The point is, it's mine. And yours too. If you want.

           [pause]

BRYN: Moon River. That's a good idea. But what you going to do with it?

CHARLEY: I might 'ave a swim in it.

BRYN: You'd drown!

CHARLEY: Why?

BRYN: I was joking!

CHARLEY: Don't joke! It's serious!

BRYN: There's nothing there.

CHARLEY: I told you, it's in my head! My imagination.

BRYN: How can you have a swim in your 'ead?

CHARLEY: That's exactly what I'm saying about the fish!

BRYN: But it's all just dreaming, Charley!

CHARLEY: No, it's not! I got loads of beautiful pictures in there. That's not dreams because they're there now. I can see them now! One thing you've got to learn if you're going to stay with me is if you want to have any say in this world you've got to make your own. My Gran told me that. So if I'm saying I'm fishing for fish it's because that's how I want to live. It can make me set out to do things.

BRYN: You know, you're like Huck Finn.

CHARLEY: [*American accent*] I was a-hankering after your sayin' that.

          [*They laugh.*]

CHARLEY: See, when I first ran away I wasn't afraid of anything. I just loved the idea of living like in the book. But the city wasn't like the book. So I came back to the river where it is. What I'm aiming is to go down Moon River and hit the Mississippi — which we call the Bristol Channel, and get to one of the islands out there.

BRYN: You know what it sounds like to me, Charley? Kid's stuff.

CHARLEY: Well, they've really got you for a sucker, haven't they? They taught you well, you think you know everything, but you don't know anything. You never even heard of the book! Well, I got things under control which is why tomorrow I'm going to the shop to get some food. Now, let's get home.

          [*Lights down.*]

SCENE SIX

[*COLIN, in disguise, comes on.*]

COLIN: I was in the village. On patrol. And I saw this girl. Dressed as a boy! I could tell she was a girl because I got a sister. I tell you, girls are dangerous but girls dressed as boys are the most dangerous things alive! So I used my nose. I knew something was wrong. I just knew that she must have something to do with Bryn. So I followed her and I found them!

[*He creeps off. Lights down.*]

SCENE SEVEN

[*The hide-out. Moonlit night. An owl hoots. Sound of hammering. Now and again we see COLIN'S spying face. BRYN is alone scoffing bread and maybe fish from a tin. After a moment or two, CHARLEY comes on. She sits. She rolls a small stick in a cigarette paper and pretends to smoke it.*]

CHARLEY: That's finished it.

BRYN: What?

CHARLEY: The boat.

BRYN: It doesn't look much like a boat.

CHARLEY: It's just a coracle.

BRYN: What's a coracle?

CHARLEY: Don't you know anything? Don't they teach you anything in school? It's a Welsh boat. A little roundish thing. It's about the last thing you'll see that's Welsh anywhere.

BRYN: Can I come with you?

CHARLEY: No.

BRYN: Why?

CHARLEY: You'd drown.

BRYN: I wouldn't.

CHARLEY: You would.

BRYN: I wouldn't!

CHARLEY: You WOULD!

[*BRYN creeps up behind CHARLEY and playfully puts his arms around her neck from behind.*]

CHARLEY: Hey, what you doing!

BRYN: Come on, Charley!

[*They 'fight' and roll around. When they come to rest, CHARLEY is on top of BRYN, pinning him down.*]

CHARLEY: Quit it, punk! O.K.?

[*BRYN is surprised at CHARLEY'S anger.*]

BRYN: O.K., Charley. O.K.!

[*Silence.*]

CHARLEY: Can you swim?

BRYN: No.

CHARLEY: There you are then. End of story. A tragedy.

[*Silence. CHARLEY goes back to 'smoking' her cigarette.*]

BRYN: That's not a fag. You're not smoking a fag.

CHARLEY: 'Course not, I don't want to get cancer.

[*Silence.*]

BRYN: You going to sail your boat down Moon River?

CHARLEY: Yeah.

BRYN: Into the Bristol Channel?

CHARLEY: No. Into the Mississippi. Know how to spell Mississippi?

BRYN: You're joking!

CHARLEY: M – i – double s – i – double s – i – double p – i. It's like a song, see? It's got a rhythm to it.

            [*CHARLEY repeats it, bouncing to the rhythm.*]

CHARLEY: You do it.

BRYN: Do it again.

            [*CHARLEY sighs. She repeats it. BRYN tries. He does it till he gets it right.*]

CHARLEY: What's got four eyes and can't see?

BRYN: I dunno. A teacher?

CHARLEY: No! Mississippi!

BRYN: I don't get it!

CHARLEY: Four i's! M – i; that's one, double s, i – that's two, double s, i – that's three, double p, i – that's four!

BRYN: I still don't get it! What can't it see?

CHARLEY: Aw shurrup, it's just a joke.

BRYN: Read some more of the book.

CHARLEY: You sure?

BRYN: I want to see if I can get it.

CHARLEY: Listen to this bit: "Now," says Ben Rogers, "what's the line of business of this gang?" "Nothing only robbery and murder," said Tom.

            [*COLIN becomes wide-eyed at 'robbery and murder'. BRYN laughs.*]

CHARLEY: [*reading*] "But who are we going to rob? Houses –

or cattle — or — stuff! Stealing cattle and such things ain't robbery, it's burglary," says Tom Sawyer. "We ain't burglars. That ain't our sort of style. We are highwaymen. We stop stages and carriages on the road, with masks on, and kill the people and take their watches and money."

"Must we always kill the people?"

"Oh, certainly. It's best."

[BRYN laughs.]

CHARLEY: "Some authorities think different, but mostly it's considered best to kill them. Except some that you bring to the cave here and keep them till they're ransomed."

"Ransomed? What's that?"

"I don't know. But that's what they do. I've seen it in books; and so of course that's what we've got to do."

"But how can we do it if we don't know what it is?"

"Why blame it all, we've GOT to do it. Don't I tell you it's in the books? So you want to go to doing different from what's in the books, and get things all muddled up?"

"Oh, that's all very fine to SAY, Tom Sawyer, but how in the nation are these fellows going to be ransomed if we don't know how to do it to them? That's the thing I want to get at. Now what do you RECKON it is?"

Do you get it now?

BRYN: Yeah. You got to do what the book says.

CHARLEY: But they don't know what it means. They are like you are now.

BRYN: [upset] It's not my fault, I just don't know.

CHARLEY: O.K. then. Listen and learn. So Tom Sawyer says.

"Well, I don't know. But per'aps if we keep them till they're ransomed, it means that we keep them till they're dead."

"Now, that's something LIKE. That'll answer. Why couldn't you said that before? We'll keep them till they're ransomed to death — and a bothersome lot they'll be, too, eating up everything and always trying to get loose."

"How you talk, Ben Rogers. How can they get loose when there's a guard over them, ready to shoot them down if they move a peg?"

"A guard. Well, that IS good. So somebody's got to set up all night and never get any sleep, just so as to watch them. I think that's foolishness. Why can't a body take a club and ransom them as soon as they get here?"

"Because it ain't in the books so — that's why. Now, Ben Rogers, do you want to do things regular, or don't you? — that's the idea. Don't you reckon that the people that made the books knows what's the correct thing to do? Do you reckon YOU can learn 'em anything? Not by a good deal. No, sir, we'll just go and ransom them in the regular way."

BRYN: But they don't know the regular way.

CHARLEY: 'Course not. 'Cause they're not interested in the regular way. They're kind of play-acting. Using their imagination. But they're making their own world. And the pirate book is helping them. Just like the book is helping me. [*reading*]

"All right. I don't mind; but I say it's a fool way, anyhow. Say — do we kill the women too?"

"Well, Ben Rogers, if I was as ignorant as you I wouldn't let on. Kill the women? No — nobody

ever saw anything in the books like that. You
fetch them to the cave, and you're always as polite
as pie to them; and by-and-by they fall in love
with you and never want to go home any more."

BRYN: E-e-e-e-e-e-h-a-a-a-a-! Ha, ha, ha!!

CHARLEY: What was that for?

BRYN: Falling in love with the women!

[*BRYN lets out another cry and makes a mildly
obscene gesture.*]

CHARLEY: What are you, some kind of male chauvinist-pig?!

BRYN: [*big man*] Yeah. Same as you!

CHARLEY: I bet you'd run a mile if a girl got closer'n the
wind in your hair to you.

BRYN: No, I wouldn't!

CHARLEY: Yes, you would.

BRYN: How do you know?

CHARLEY: I can tell.

BRYN: [*hurt*] So? I bet you've never been with a girl
either! Have you?

CHARLEY: You want to hear some more of this?

BRYN: Come on, Charley! Tell me! You ever been with a
girl?

CHARLEY: No, I ain't! Now, you want a bit more?

BRYN: Well, I'll be! Big Charley Huck Finn he ain't never
had a woman! Well, I'll be!

CHARLEY: O.K. Cut it out! [*reading*]

"And by the by they fall in love with you and
never want to go home any more."

"Well, if that's the way, I'm agreed, but I don't
take no stock in it. Mighty soon we'll have the

cave so cluttered up with women, and fellows waiting to be ransomed, that there won't be no place for the robbers."

[*BRYN laughs.*]

CHARLEY: "But go ahead, I ain't got nothing to say."

"Little Tommy Barnes was asleep, now, and when they waked him up he was scared, and cried, and said he wanted to go home to his Ma, and didn't want to be a robber any more."

BRYN: Aw, poor kid! Ha, ha!

CHARLEY: Yeah, it's sort of sad.

"So they all made fun of him, and called him cry-baby, and that made him mad, and he said he would go straight and tell all the secrets. But Tom give him five cents to keep quiet, and said we would all go home and meet next week and rob somebody and kill some people."

"Ben Rogers said he couldn't get out much, only Sundays, and so he wanted to begin next Sunday; but all the boys said it would be wicked to do it on Sunday, and that settled the thing. They agreed to get together and fix a day as soon as they could, and then we elected Tom Sawyer first captain and Joe Harper second captain of the Gang, and so started home."

"I climb up the shed and crept into my window just before day was breaking. My new clothes was all greased up and clayey, and I was dog-tired."

BRYN: That's a great book!

CHARLEY: My Gran gave it to me.

BRYN: You wouldn't think a book like that would be allowed, would you, with kids talking about killing and robbing?

CHARLEY: No! But that's the point. Where'd kids get those words from? From the grown-ups. Only here's the difference. Kids don't do it. Grown-ups do. That's what's so good about the book. It shows that if kids run things there might be a lot of talk but it wouldn't come to nothing. All it comes to is giving Tommy Barnes five cents not to tell. It wouldn't come to actually slicing off the parts of people's bodies.

BRYN: Shurrup, Charley, I just eaten!

CHARLEY: But kids don't run the world. So they have to make up their own. But not in any stupid or childish way; according to the book. If kids ever took to really killing, it's 'cos they'd give up books. The book shows you how awesome you are, that's all.

BRYN: Awesome?

CHARLEY: Yeah. Like, whenever kids do anything that's serious, grown-ups think they're playing. They always want to make it seem like nothing so that what THEY tell you to do looks like the real thing. But what they call playing, is the real thing for kids. It's what we WANT to do. It's what's important. 'Cos we're not playing. We're making something. That's what the book is about. And we've got to have weapons. Like imagination. Imagine something and you can DO something. It's cosmic, kid.

BRYN: I think I get it now.

CHARLEY: Another weapon is the teacher trap.

BRYN: The teacher trap? What's that?

CHARLEY: Well, it's like a man-trap only it's for teachers and others. But it don't kill them. It just ties them up for a while. Long enough to get away. It's just to stop them getting too close.

BRYN: Where is it?

CHARLEY: Near. It's in the woods. I've made it look as if the path is going into the bushes but that's just camouflage. What happens is, you go into the bushes and fall down the bank onto your bum! So simple. Anyway, it's time to get your head down.

            [*They lay down. Owl hoots.*]

BRYN: It's funny, Charley, I'm not scared. Not even with the owl. I feel like I'm in a gang like Tom Sawyer's; that could kill and bomb and rob and no one could hurt me!

            [*COLIN'S face looks suddenly fearful. He leaves.*]

BRYN: [*startled*] What's that!

CHARLEY: Ha, ha! You're just as scared as ever! You're just a kid! It was probably a cat!

            [*Silence.*]

CHARLEY: [*spookily*] Or a bear. Or a mad-man with a big axe.

BRYN: Shurrup, Charley! Why can't we go inside!

CHARLEY: Because of my boat!

BRYN: But there's room.

CHARLEY: Yeah, but I want the boat to get a good night's rest.

            [*Silence*]

BRYN: Charley.

            [*CHARLEY sighs deeply.*]

CHARLEY: Yeah?

BRYN: Sing that song your Gran taught you.

CHARLEY: [*singing*] Moon River, wider than a mile
            I'm crossing you in style someday
            we're after the same rainbow's end

waiting round the bend
my Huckleberry friend
Moon River and me.

That's it.

BRYN: You've got a good voice for a kid. I mean, you know, a boy kid.

[*Silence. Lights down.*]

SCENE EIGHT

[*A schoolroom. COLIN and MISS.*]

COLIN: Miss, Miss, Miss! They're terrorists! They're going to kill people. Miss!

MISS: Who, Colin?

COLIN: Bryn, Miss.

MISS: Bryn? Brynley Morgan?

COLIN: Yes, Miss!

MISS: You've seen him?!

COLIN: Yes, Miss!

MISS: Where?

COLIN: I — I don't know, Miss.

MISS: You don't know?

COLIN: No, Miss, it was dark, I was scared. I ran, Miss, they've got guns and bombs, Miss.

MISS: Who?!

COLIN: Brynley, Miss! And his friend!

MISS: Which friend?

[*COLIN is silent.*]

MISS: Colin?

COLIN: I can't say, Miss.

MISS: Why?

COLIN: Because... because, I don't know.

MISS: You don't know who it is?

COLIN: No.

MISS: Have you told the police?

COLIN: No, Miss!

MISS: Why?

COLIN: I don't know where Brynley is!

MISS: Perhaps it wouldn't be a good idea at this point anyway. If the police get involved Brynley may find out and run away before we can even speak to him. You'll have to take me.

COLIN: But you won't get near, Miss! They've got a teacher trap, Miss!

MISS: A what?!

COLIN: A teacher trap!

MISS: What is it?

COLIN: I don't know!

MISS: But you don't know anything!

COLIN: Miss, Miss! They're near the river! I remember now, I heard it.

            [*Silence. A bell rings.*]

MISS: Go for your dinner now, Colin. Come and see me later.

            [*COLIN leaves. MISS sits in thought. Lights go down. A bell rings. Lights up. COLIN comes on.*]

MISS: I've thought of something, Colin. Sit for a

moment. Let me tell you.

[*COLIN sits.*]

MISS: There was once a particular tribe of Indians living in the Amazon forest — the Amazon is a river. Some white men from the city wanted to make contact with them...

COLIN: Miss, is this a story?

MISS: In a sense, Colin. Colin, are you old enough to think responsibly?

COLIN: I don't see what you mean, Miss.

MISS: Well, imaginatively. You see I thought of these Indians after you told me about Brynley. If I tell YOU about them perhaps it will mean something to you. I mean something about their story may give you an idea that we can follow. A way that we might deal with the situation.

COLIN: I'll give it a go, Miss.

MISS: Good. Now, the white men knew that this tribe had never left this part of the forest. For the tribe, it was their whole world. THE whole world. The white people brought pots and pans and hung them on the branches of trees around the village. The Indians had never seen anything like these pots and pans before. So they collected them and took them back to the village. Then the next day, there was something else hanging from the branches. And the day after something else again. This went on for a few more days until one day the Indians came out of the village only now there were no THINGS but people. White people. The people who had put the pots and pans there in the first place. And the Indians trusted them. It was the sheer surprise of finding these things hanging in the branches. It was all so strange that they had never even been able to put together a simple question about it. Like: where did they come from? It was all so surprising that the Indians weren't even able to consider what it might mean.

[*Pause.*]

COLIN: Maybe that's it, Miss! That's how we can get them up from the river! Leave something out.

MISS: Like what?

COLIN: I don't know. Food?

MISS: Good, yes. Do you mean something like a loaf of bread?

COLIN: I don't know.

MISS: It's just that... well, if it was something they could smell then perhaps the SMELL of it might lure them up from the river.

COLIN: That's a great idea! Yeah! But what?

MISS: Well, I've got one of those little barbecues at home. We could use that.

COLIN: It makes sense, Miss! The way Brynley was eating was like... like he was a prisoner on a Devil's Island! He must've been so hungry! And I was so scared, Miss. There was an owl. And it just seemed awful. In the moonlight.

MISS: Well they obviously have little food. [*pause*] I think what you and I should do, young Mr Pope, is go down that path tomorrow and make a little fire and barbecue a few aromatic items of meat!

COLIN: Yummy, Miss! And don't tell anyone?

MISS: No, I don't think so. We need to make contact first.

COLIN: And we'll have to watch out for the teacher trap!

MISS: Hmmm!

[*Pause.*]

COLIN: Miss?

MISS: Yes?

COLIN: What happened to the Indians?

MISS: It was actually very sad. They let the white people in. But eventually the white people moved THEM out. You see, they surprised them again. They took them for a ride in a boat on the river. And they never brought them back. But one day years later some of the Indians did return and what they found was that their village was gone. Everything about their lives and its culture that they'd built up over many years had gone. And the whole place had been bulldozed and excavated. You see, the white man had found gold. Under their village. There was gold beneath the village, beneath this world of the Indians and it had always been there. But gold would have been pretty useless to the Indians. You can't eat it, you can't grow it and though you could build a hut with it there are much more practical materials for that: in the forest around them.

[*Pause.*]

COLIN: That IS sad, Miss.

MISS: Yes. Without their world they were lost. They became useless. They turned to drink and other things and died away. It's a lesson, Colin. It shows that there is such a thing as false trust.

COLIN: FALSE trust, Miss?

MISS: Yes. Trust is like... well it's like a deal made between people. But such a deal can only be made when both sides are strong. And that can only happen when both sides KNOW all the facts. That's why education is so important. You need to get to know the things that will make you strong.

COLIN: I suppose you're right!

MISS: Go on then, Colin.

COLIN: O.K., Miss! Tara, Miss.

[*COLIN leaves. MISS picks up a telephone and dials. She waits for an answer.*]

MISS: Mr Morgan? This is Brynley's teacher. We think we know where Brynley is. [*pause*] Oh, yes, he's safe. [*pause*] Yes, it is good. But we don't know precisely. I haven't told the police because we don't want Brynley to be frightened away again. [*pause*] Well I think it's been just a bit of a prank. Or perhaps not a prank but... well, children tend to exaggerate, Mr Morgan. They blow things up out of all proportion. [*pause*] Well if we know precisely where he was I would agree. But we don't. So I'm going to look for him tomorrow morning and feel quite positive about finding him. [*pause*] Yes, I know Mr Morgan. But consider this: if he becomes frightened he may do something that could endanger his life. [*pause*] Yes, of course I will. I'll phone you as soon as possible. [*pause*] Yes. [*pause*] Bye, bye, Mr Morgan.

[*She puts the phone down. Lights down.*]

SCENE NINE

[*The path. BRYN and CHARLEY back onto stage looking off the way they've come (at the teacher trap).*]

CHARLEY: That's it. The teacher trap.

BRYN: It's awesome, Charley!

[*BRYN suddenly stops and turns around with his nose in the air.*]

BRYN: Smell that!

93

CHARLEY: What?

BRYN: Burgers!

CHARLEY: Burgers?

BRYN: Barbecue burgers! And ONIONS!

CHARLEY: Out here? Not possible! It's your imagination!

BRYN: It's not, Charley! I feel as if I've got a whole Wimpy up my nose! Let's go and look! It could be some kids. We could ambush them!

CHARLEY: You know what it smells like to me?

BRYN: What?

CHARLEY: Danger.

BRYN: Aw, come on, Charley!

            [BRYN begins to go off towards 'smell'.]

CHARLEY: I saw this programme! About some Indians! They lost their whole village because they were fooled by something unusual! Well I'm not going to be fooled! If it's unusual it's just BECAUSE it's unusual!

            [BRYN goes off, nose in air.]

CHARLEY: Dummy!

            [CHARLEY waits looking off then walks to go off the way they came on, then stops and goes back towards the 'smell'. Suddenly there is a commotion. CHARLEY rushes off. BRYN runs across the stage pursued by MISS and COLIN. BRYN runs off. BRYN cries out, off. MISS and COLIN stop, looking off with their mouths agape. Silence.]

SCENE TEN

[*The police station. A room. BRYN is sitting with his head bowed. He has plasters on facial cuts. He is in (plastic) handcuffs. COLIN comes on.*]

COLIN: I'll take them off now.

BRYN: You're a rat, Colin!

COLIN: Why? Why?

BRYN: Putting these on me.

COLIN: They said I could. They said if you wanted to play cops and robbers then this is what happens.

BRYN: I never played at robbing anyone! It was a dirty, stinking trick to put these on me!

COLIN: Ah, come on, Bryn! I was only joking!

           [*He takes handcuffs off.*]

COLIN: Hey, you know that kid you were with?

BRYN: [*excited*] Yeah, tell me! He made it, didn't he?

COLIN: Made it?

BRYN: Yeah! Down the river in the cockle!

COLIN: Cockle?!

           [*BRYN throws his arm into the air in a victory salute.*]

BRYN: Yeah! I know it! He made it.

COLIN: The kid was picked up getting on a bus for Cardiff!

BRYN: [*with disbelief*] What? You're lying to me, Colin. He could do it. He said he could do it and that's what I believe.

COLIN: And also, that kid was a girl!

BRYN: A girl!

COLIN: Yeah. So how'd you expect a girl to make it down the river! Her name is Charlotte.

BRYN: Charlotte!

COLIN: Yeah.

BRYN: [*shocked*] A girl!

COLIN: So you never had snogs with her then?

BRYN: [*horrified*] What! Shut your face, Colin! You're nothing but a male showing-off pig! And you're a spy!

COLIN: I'm the deputy!

BRYN: What d'you mean?

COLIN: I got to find out certain things. If you don't tell ME, they'll GRILL you.

BRYN: GRILL me?!

COLIN: Yeah, That's what they said to say.

BRYN: What? Like a barbecue?

COLIN: I s'pose so.

BRYN: You're having me on!

COLIN: No, I'm not!

BRYN: You're just jealous, Colin, 'cos I stayed out in the nights with a GIRL!

COLIN: But you thought she was a boy!

BRYN: So? Anyway, how do you know? I just IMAGINED she was a boy! You're no deputy, Colin. You're just imagining it. But there's a difference between using your imagination to make a poem of your life and using your imagination to pretend something. Like being a deputy. I'm not afraid of you!

[*BRYN suddenly grabs COLIN'S nose. COLIN cries out.*]

BRYN: You started it, Colin. You made me write on your blotting paper, didn't you?

COLIN: Lay off, Bryn!

BRYN: It was like getting me to do something dirty on your life, Colin. Because your life is like a piece of blotting paper, Charley told me that! It was all your fault!

[*BRYN twists COLIN'S nose. COLIN cries out.*]

BRYN: You should be more careful about your own things, Colin, or one day you lose everything. Everything that's valuable. Like your nose. And the truth!

[*BRYN twists COLIN'S nose again.*]

COLIN: Leave off, Bryn!

BRYN: So tell the truth! Tell it was your fault!

COLIN: O.K.! O.K., Bryn.

[*BRYN lets go of COLIN'S nose. COLIN holds his nose.*]

COLIN: You needn't have done that. Just 'cos you think you're some kind of hero.

[*BRYN suddenly points at COLIN as though with a sword.*]

BRYN: You! [*pause*] Asked for it!

[*Silence.*]

BRYN: Sorry?

COLIN: Yeah, course I am! [*He sniffs.*] Bryn?

BRYN: Yeah?

COLIN: Friends?

BRYN: 'Course!

COLIN: Shake on it?

[*They shake hands with COLIN still holding his nose. COLIN goes off. BRYN'S MUM comes on. She rushes to BRYN and hugs him.*]

MUM: You're a naughty boy, Brynley Morgan! I've got a good mind to... Do you know how worried your father? ... It's a good job that the police have got a sense... Look at your face all... Where were you when they?...

BRYN: Mum?

MUM: Yes? What?

BRYN: If I leave it up to you all to teach me, how do I know you're going to teach me what's going to help me to KNOW what to do rather than what's going to help you all MAKE me do?

[*BRYN'S MUM looks at him with mouth hanging wide. Silence. Lights down.*]

SCENE ELEVEN

[*The home of the BENNETT-JONESES. CHARLEY is dressed as before: as a boy. She is with MR BENNETT-JONES. Both look uncomfortable.*]

MR B-J: What you don't understand, Charlotte...

CHARLEY: Charley.

MR B-J: ...Charley, is that... we love you. A child needs the love and safety of a home. I want a child to hold and care for. I want a child who needs me!

[*MRS BENNETT-JONES comes on. She stands in silence for a moment. She has been crying. Both the others look at her — a little in awe.*]

MRS B-J: Oh, Charley, how could you have done this to us?! I know now what a child needs! A child needs discipline. Her life must be ordered. She must be told what to do: what to think.

[*She looks to her husband.*]

MR B-J: Yes, that and she must be given security.

[*In the following speech CHARLEY nods negatively.*]

MRS B-J: Yes, Charley. You must have been terrified out there at night. Away from HOME. Away from the protection of people who love you. At the mercy of the elements and evil cruel people. No? How can you say 'no', Charley, when you know it's true?

[*MRS BENNETT-JONES takes hold of CHARLEY.*]

MRS B-J: Tell me you were afraid! Tell me!

CHARLEY: I wasn't!

MR B-J: Mair! We don't want the child to be afraid of US! Charley! Show some respect! Tell Mrs B-J what she wants to hear!

[*CHARLEY gets up as if to leave.*]

CHARLEY: But that's it! You only want me to say that because it makes you feel better! Like you want to give me security to lock me up not to protect me! What you want to do is civilise me. This is what Huck calls it. You want to make me like you. To me, that's tragic. I don't want to be like you! I want to be like me! If I'm like you then I've got to give up being like me! And if you give up being like you there's no point in being like anyone! I want to be like me and use my IMAGINATION in being like me. So I lit out. Left home. But it didn't make me afraid. It made me feel strong!

[*Silence.*]

MR B-J: Would you like to live with us, Charley?

CHARLEY: Are you going to want me to wear a dress? A skirt?

MRS B-J: It would be nice. Occasionally.

            [*Pause.*]

CHARLEY: We've got to make a deal.

            [*Lights down.*]

SCENE TWELVE

[*Sound of river. BRYN is sitting, reading from a book. MISS comes on.*]

MISS: Brynley? Why are you down here?

BRYN: Dunno, Miss.

MISS: Is it Charley?

BRYN: Dunno, Miss.

MISS: I'm sure you'll get to see her again. Someday. That would be good, wouldn't it?

            [*Silence.*]

MISS: Brynley?

            [*Silence.*]

MISS: I want to say sorry, Brynley. I... I shouldn't have called you a liar. No one should call a child a liar. It breaks the trust. The trust that we need to build between a child and its life. I'm sorry. I learned a good lesson.

BRYN: It's O.K., Miss.

MISS: I teach and I often forget to learn. Though in the case of grown-ups it's more a case of the need to unlearn. Of unlearning bad habits. Like taking children for granted and always thinking that WE know what they need. Like I know that you need to see Charley.

BRYN: Miss, I don't, Miss!

MISS: What?

BRYN: She cheated, Miss! She made me believe she could sail down the river into the sea!

MISS: Brynley. How many people do you think could do that? REALLY?

            [*Silence.*]

MISS: You should go home soon.

            [*MISS goes. CHARLEY comes on and sneaks up behind him. She's wearing girl's clothes. She suddenly puts her hands around his eyes.*]

BRYN: Colin! Gerroff! You'll push me into the river!

            [*CHARLEY laughs. She takes her hands away. BRYN looks at her in wonder. He's suddenly embarrassed.*]

CHARLEY: What's the matter, kid?

            [*She sits next to him.*]

CHARLEY: Want a fag?

            [*She offers him a pretend cigarette. They smoke, inhaling deeply.*]

CHARLEY: Nothing like smoking fresh river air.

            [*Silence.*]

CHARLEY: Did they give you a rough time? Third degree, all that?

BRYN: What do you mean?

CHARLEY: You know. Did they grill you?

BRYN: [*bitterly*] What do you mean? Like a slice of bacon?

            [*Silence.*]

BRYN: Colin admitted that it was really his fault. He said how he'd made it up about us being terrorists.

CHARLEY: The kid's got some imagination! Maybe we should get him into our gang!

BRYN: Why should anyone want to be in our gang when you tell LIES!

CHARLEY: Lies? [*pause*] Oh, I get it. Me being a girl. Well let me tell you, kid, you try being a girl sometime. There are things you can't do 'cos it's expected GIRLS can't do them. You know: all that sexist stuff.

BRYN: I'm not talking about that. I'm talking about you didn't go down the river in a boat. So what good did the book do? All that talk. You're just like the teachers!

CHARLEY: One difference: I CHOSE the book.

BRYN: You didn't! Your Gran did!

CHARLEY: O.K., O.K.! But don't think that books can solve all your problems. They just help. They can't make the plan you need but they can show you you need a plan!

BRYN: What plan!

CHARLEY: A deal! Kids have got to make a deal between themselves and grown-ups. But they can only do that if they can think for themselves. That's where the book comes in. So I may not have got down the river but I sure made a deal!

[*She draws deep on her 'cigarette' and inhales happily.*]

BRYN: So have you been adopted?

CHARLEY: Sort of. Only they didn't adopt me, I adopted them. It cost me, of course. [*She stands up.*] Behold me, kid! You ever seen such a thing? Huck Finn in a skirt? That's the deal!

[*They laugh.*]

CHARLEY: But also I get to smoke as much as I want to.

BRYN: Yeah?

CHARLEY: Sure. Another part of the deal is that they allow
            me to be sensible and responsible enough for my
            own life to know that smoking kills you but
            smoking fresh air don't!

            [*She sits again.*]

BRYN: [*happily*] You know, Charley, I think you know
            more than my Mum and Dad!

CHARLEY: Well it's funny you should say that, kid. My Gran
            told me this: the child is father to the man. It was
            written by a famous poet, a guy called Words-
            worth.

BRYN: That's a funny name.

CHARLEY: Words ought to be worth something anyway.

BRYN: Yeah. Say it again.

CHARLEY: The child is father to the man.

BRYN: I don't get it.

CHARLEY: Don't get it! Hey, you're looking at the mother of
            the Bennett-Joneses! It's just what you said. You
            gotta educate them. How are they going to know
            how to treat us lessen we tell 'em!

            [*They laugh.*]

CHARLEY: You know, I was surprised.

BRYN: What?

CHARLEY: One thing I never thought.

BRYN: What?

CHARLEY: They missed me.

            [*Pause.*]

BRYN: So did I, Charley.

CHARLEY: Yeah?

BRYN: Yeah.

CHARLEY: I suppose you're kind of a cute little kid. I got to go. O.K.?

BRYN: Yeah. Hey, Charley.

CHARLEY: Yeah?

BRYN: Don't patronise me. That would be tragic.

[*Pause.*]

CHARLEY: Yeah, O.K., kid. [*pause*] So. Give us a kiss.

[*Pause. BRYN kisses her on the cheek.*]

CHARLEY: Not there, dummy! On the lips!

[*CHARLEY takes BRYN'S head and kisses him on the lips.*

[*Lights down.*]

David

Notes to the Original Production

David was commissioned by Spectacle Theatre with support from the Arts Council of Wales. This play was first performed on February 5, 1996 at Pontygwaith Primary, Rhondda Fach.

Directed by	Steve Davis
Designed by	James Denton
Stage Manager	Sian Llewellyn

Cast

David	Martin Jago
Leah/David's Mother	Gwenno Penrhyn
Goliath/Elijah	
& Goliath's Father	Brendan Charleson

Act One
SCENE ONE

[*The home of DAVID. DAVID and his MOTHER. MOTHER is close to tears.*]

MOTHER: David?

DAVID: What, Mum?

MOTHER: Come here.

DAVID: What?

MOTHER: Come here, David. Come here.

DAVID: O.K.

MOTHER: Let me hold you.

DAVID: What's the matter?

MOTHER: I just need to hold you.

DAVID: O.K.

[*MOTHER hugs DAVID.*]

DAVID: Don't let Dad see you. It winds him up.

MOTHER: It's what I need.

DAVID: What's the matter, Mum? What's the matter?

MOTHER: I feel a bit depressed. That's all. Just a bit.

DAVID: Why?

MOTHER: No reason. There's no real reason. It just happens. Just comes.

DAVID: It makes you feel better to tell me?

MOTHER: Yes.

DAVID: I'm glad.

MOTHER: Sometimes I feel so afraid.

DAVID: Of what?

MOTHER: I don't know. It's wrong. I shouldn't talk to you like this. There's nothing to be afraid of really. It's just me.

DAVID: It's Dad.

MOTHER: No.

DAVID: It is. It makes me depressed too.

MOTHER: No! You see, son? I shouldn't have started.

DAVID: I'm going out.

FATHER: [off] Ruth!

[MOTHER goes to off.]

MOTHER: [to off] What?

FATHER: [off] Get me a can!

MOTHER: [to off] Wait a minute! I'm talking to David. [to DAVID] Where are you going?

DAVID: My friend's.

MOTHER: What friend?

DAVID: Elijah.

MOTHER: He's too old for you.

DAVID: He's not that old. He's helping me with the guitar.

MOTHER: He's only helped you.

DAVID: That's what I said.

MOTHER: You'd better watch things.

DAVID: Watch what?

MOTHER: Don't go experimenting.

DAVID: Experimenting? With what?

MOTHER: Things.

DAVID: What, you mean sex and drugs?

MOTHER: Alright. Sex and drugs.

           [*DAVID picks up his guitar. While they speak he tunes it.*]

DAVID: Don't be daft, Mum.

MOTHER: I'd better get that can.

FATHER: [*off*] Ruth!

MOTHER: [*off*] I'm getting it, Mo!

           [*She goes off. DAVID begins picking a tune. MOTHER comes back on with can.*]

MOTHER: People do experiment. Especially at your age.

DAVID: The only thing we experiment with is...

           [*MOTHER goes off with can. DAVID goes on picking. MOTHER returns.*]

DAVID: ...is Jesus.

MOTHER: Jesus?

DAVID: That's exactly how he says it: you don't need to experiment with anything. Just Jesus. Jesus is the only drug you need.

MOTHER: This Elijah?

DAVID: Yes.

MOTHER: What is he, a nutter?

DAVID: I don't think he's sure what he is.

MOTHER: He sounds like a Mooney!

DAVID: At the moment I think he's a Rasta. You know. Like Bob Marley.

MOTHER: He's not a lunatic is he, David? How hold is he?

DAVID: Nineteen.

MOTHER: And he lives on his own?

DAVID: Yes.

MOTHER: Why isn't he living at home?

DAVID: Because he doesn't want to be a burden. He says.

MOTHER: D'you want some bread and marge?

DAVID: No thanks.

MOTHER: Your father wants some. He'll have a crisp sandwich. While he's watching Cardiff.

DAVID: What a waste of time, Mum! Cardiff always lose!

MOTHER: It's all he's got.

DAVID: What's all he's got? Watching Cardiff lose?

MOTHER: It's all he's got since he lost his job. It's all most of the men around here have got.

DAVID: But it's nothing!

MOTHER: It's nothing because the only something he had was his work. When that work went he was left with nothing.

DAVID: Jesus could be something.

MOTHER: No he couldn't! How could he be? He can't give your Dad a job. I think it would be a very sad thing, David, if, because he can't get a job down here on earth he tries to make touch with a God in heaven he doesn't even know is there, just to comfort himself!

DAVID: I didn't say God.

[*MOTHER takes bread and marge off. DAVID picks at*

tune. MOTHER comes back on.]

MOTHER: David, I'm worried about you.

[*She sits near DAVID. She holds his face.*]

MOTHER: I don't want you becoming a Jesus freak. A Jesus child. You're mine. I don't want to lose you. This is what happens when people get depressed. They turn to Jesus in their droves.

DAVID: It's alright, Mum! There's nothing to worry about.

MOTHER: When I was a kid I couldn't take to Jesus. I had friends who loved him. But I didn't like it that he said we were sheep and he was our shepherd! We're not sheep! We don't want to be sheep! All the men were once the coal board's sheep. The head of the South Wales Coal Board was their shepherd. Look where it got them!

[*Pause.*]

DAVID: I don't know anything about that, Mum. The coal mines were closed before I was born.

MOTHER: Not all of them. There was one. For a while the men held onto it like a life-line. As if that was a prayer. [*as an afterthought:*] To Jesus.

[*Silence.*]

DAVID: Listen to this, Mum.

MOTHER: What is it?

DAVID: I made it up.

[*DAVID plays and sings the following:*]

DAVID: Let me sing this simple song
it is what I can do
let it fill the whole night long
when I get to feeling blue.

MOTHER: Clever. You wrote that?

DAVID: [*as though she hadn't spoken*]
Let me play my simple tune
in a world where music's gone,
this is what I can do
let me sing my simple song.

FATHER: [*from off, but closer as though standing in doorway*]
Ruth! What's that ruddy noise? I'm trying to watch Cardiff!

[*Silence. DAVID hangs his head.*]

MOTHER: I'm sorry, love.

[*DAVID gets up angrily. He takes his guitar and goes.*]

MOTHER: [*holding out a hand after him*] David!

[*Lights down.*]

SCENE TWO

[*ELIJAH'S room. ELIJAH is like a hippy. (Maybe he has dreadlocks?) There could be joss sticks, etc. ELIJAH is sitting cross-legged. He's listening to DAVID playing his guitar. He plays a short piece of music. DAVID stops.*]

ELIJAH: [*with a West-Indian accent*] You play better than me now. I can't teach you any more.

DAVID: My Mother's worried.

ELIJAH: About what?

DAVID: Jesus.

ELIJAH: Your mother's worried about Jesus? She shouldn't be. He can look after himself.

DAVID: I think that's what she's worried about.

ELIJAH: What?

112

DAVID

DAVID: Talking about him as if he was alive.

ELIJAH: He is, man!

DAVID: He's been dead two thousand years.

ELIJAH: He's not alive like that. It's silly to even try and talk about it in the way we talk about things being dead or alive. I suppose you're having doubts now.

DAVID: Not really.

ELIJAH: Good. I'll tell you how he lives. HE lives inside you. That's why you shouldn't smoke.

DAVID: Why?

ELIJAH: Because you could choke him.

DAVID: That's daft, Lije! He's not living in me! And how could he live in everybody? There must be a lot of people who wouldn't want him inside them. What about Japanese people?

ELIJAH: There are Japanese Christians.

DAVID: You know what I mean. Do you think he'd want to be inside somebody if they didn't want him?

ELIJAH: He only lives in you if you ask him in. Obviously what I'm talking about is the spirit of things. It's the idea of Him that you take in. So if you smoke you're not really choking him but the idea of him. Because the idea of him is to love you. And if He loves you you should at least respect yourself and how can you do that if you're deliberately taking into yourself something that can give you cancer?

          [*Silence.*]

DAVID: My Mum loves me.

ELIJAH: O.K.

DAVID: Why should I need Jesus if I've got my Mum?

ELIJAH: I don't know. You tell me. It's for you to decide. Play something.

[*DAVID picks. While DAVID plays, ELIJAH does a dance with the top half of his body.*]

DAVID: [*still picking*] Can you see the point of supporting Cardiff?

ELIJAH: [*still dancing*] What?

DAVID: Cardiff City Football Club.

ELIJAH: Not my scene, man.

DAVID: It's not mine either but my Dad supports Cardiff and they always lose. One day they'll lose for the last time and then Cardiff won't have a football club. What'll happen to my Dad then?

ELIJAH: Do you want the good news or the bad news first?

DAVID: Don't joke, Lije!

ELIJAH: O.K. You got a girlfriend? No, you're too young.

DAVID: As a matter of fact I have.

ELIJAH: You have? Who is she?

DAVID: Well. Her name is Leah.

ELIJAH: O.K. There's your answer.

DAVID: Where?

[*David stops playing.*]

ELIJAH: If Cardiff City dies it's because they're not needed. Not even by your Dad. As long as there's one lonely supporter, Cardiff City will live on. So if they die it's because even your Dad has given up.

DAVID: What's that got to do with Leah?

ELIJAH: She's your girlfriend! She's your girlfriend because you need her! If you didn't need her she wouldn't be your girlfriend! Same with Jesus. He

DAVID

exists because people need him.

DAVID: I'm too young for this!

ELIJAH: Don't put yourself down, man! Mozart wrote his first symphony when he was four! Play that tune again. I was just getting into the rhythm!

[*DAVID plays, ELIJAH sways. Lights down.*]

SCENE THREE

[*A mountain top. There is a rock of some kind behind which GOLIATH is hiding as scene begins. LEAH comes on. She has a flower.*]

LEAH: [*to AUDIENCE*] I've got a flower. A rose is a rose is a rose. It's the line of a poem. What does it mean? All roses are roses? A rose is not a hyacinth? A flower has a name. A name makes something. That's a girl's name. Daisy. Another girl's name. Why don't flowers have boys' names? I call my flower... [*pause*] Fred. Doesn't sound right. [*pause*] Alan. Doesn't sound right! It's not fair! If we don't give flowers boys' names then we don't give boys flowers' names. But then that lets people use the names in a way they shouldn't. Nastily. Like calling a boy Pansy. Maybe because he's gentle. Graceful. Like a girl. I don't know. It's something to think about. What about believing in something? That's called religion. Could it happen in the same way? Could somebody call somebody else something just to get at them? I think that would be well bad. Christian or Muslim or Hindu. Protestant or Catholic. Why should it be different? They all believe! A rose is a rose is a rose. Well cool! A believer is a believer is a believer. Maybe we should call our religions after ourselves! I'm a Leah-ist. Like a Buddhist. A

115

Davidian. Like a Christian. A... no! Why? Maybe we should just believe in ourselves! A flower is a flower is a flower! Anyway it's something to think about. And what if you don't believe in anything? Not even a flower?

[*There is crying from off. It gets louder. LEAH hides. GOLIATH comes on in a wretched state. He falls where LEAH was. He cries and hits the floor. LEAH comes on carefully. She stops over him. (She doesn't now have the flower.)*]

LEAH: Goliath?

[*GOLIATH immediately stops crying and wipes his face out of sight of her.*]

LEAH: Gol? What's the matter?

[*Silence.*]

LEAH: Gol?

GOLIATH: What?

LEAH: What's the matter?

GOLIATH: What's the matter with what?

LEAH: With you.

GOLIATH: Nothing!

LEAH: So why're you crying?

GOLIATH: I'm not crying!

LEAH: Let's see your face.

GOLIATH: No.

LEAH: Why?

GOLIATH: I don't want you to see it.

LEAH: 'Cos of the tears?

GOLIATH: No! 'Cos I'm ugly.

LEAH: Ugly?

GOLIATH: Yeah. I got an ugly face.

            [*LEAH kneels beside him.*]

LEAH: Flipping heck, Gol! That's sad! You haven't got an ugly face! Who said that?

GOLIATH: Someone did.

LEAH: Is that why you're crying?

GOLIATH: I'm not!

LEAH: O.K.

            [*LEAH sits behind him. LEAH starts singing.*]

LEAH: Johnny Depp he's my love
            he's well cool like the Lord above...

GOLIATH: Who's Johnny Depp?

LEAH: Edward Scissorhands!

GOLIATH: Hmmm. Well, it's a stupid song.

LEAH: David made it up for me.

GOLIATH: He gets on my nerves. David. He thinks he's so clever. He's just a swot.

            [*Silence. GOLIATH lays on his back supporting himself on his elbows. LEAH hums tune of song.*]

GOLIATH: I enjoy being ignorant.

LEAH: What?

GOLIATH: I like being ignorant.

LEAH: That's well mad, Gol.

GOLIATH: Don't be daft. Think of all the time it gives me for doing things.

LEAH: What time?

GOLIATH: All the time I've got when I'm not trying to learn something so I won't be ignorant.

LEAH: But you don't do anything! You just lay around!

GOLIATH: So what? That's what I like doing!

LEAH: Pick me a flower.

GOLIATH: Pick you a flower where? There's no flowers here. It's a bare mountain!

LEAH: Alright. I bet there's one flower somewhere! Go and look for it. For me! Then it won't matter if you are ignorant. You'll be kind.

GOLIATH: Shut up, Leah! You don't know anything about being ignorant! You're ignorant about it!

LEAH: Ignorant about being ignorant?

GOLIATH: Yeah. You can't just be ignorant! You've gotta know what you're doing!

LEAH: It shouldn't stop you from being able to go and get me a flower.

[*Silence.*]

LEAH: What you doing?

GOLIATH: I'm having to think about it. [*pause*] Have you ever heard the word lummux?

LEAH: What is it?

GOLIATH: I don't know! It's a word.

LEAH: Did someone call you it?

GOLIATH: [*angrily*] As a matter of fact, no!

LEAH: Alright, there's no need to get airiated.

GOLIATH: Airiated? What's that?

LEAH: This is your trouble, Gol. Your ignorance makes you ignorant. You don't know anything. [*pause*] Did your Mum call you a lummux? That's well sad.

GOLIATH: No.

LEAH: Your Dad?

GOLIATH: Look! What's it got to do with you?!

LEAH: Sorry, Gol.

[*Silence.*]

GOLIATH: Leah?

LEAH: Yeah?

GOLIATH: Will you go with me?

[*Silence.*]

GOLIATH: Leah?

LEAH: I don't know. I'm thinking. [*pause*] Just go and see if you can find me a flower. Show how nice you can be. Go over there. [*She indicates where she hid.*] You might find something.

GOLIATH: If I get you one will you go with me?

LEAH: See if you can get a flower first.

[*GOLIATH gets up and goes off. LEAH lays back happily. DAVID comes on with his guitar. LEAH starts with a gasp.*]

LEAH: Dave! What are you doing here?

DAVID: Hiya, Leah! I just come up here to practise. What you doing here?

LEAH: Nothing. I was just going. [*aside*] This is well serious!

DAVID: Don't go. I was just going to sit down with you.

[*He sits.*]

LEAH: I've got to go, Dave.

[*She begins to get up. GOLIATH comes on excitedly. He's carrying LEAH'S flower.*]

GOLIATH: Look, Leah! I found a flower!

[*LEAH groans. DAVID looks surprised.*]

GOLIATH: [*to DAVID*] What you doing here?

LEAH: He was just passing.

GOLIATH: On a mountaintop? Get lost, Evans.

DAVID: No. Why?

GOLIATH: 'Cos otherwise I'll beat your face in. She's going with me.

DAVID: What's he on about, Leah?

LEAH: I dunno. Shurrup, Gol. I'm not going out with you. Dave is my boyfriend.

[*Silence. GOLIATH crumples up flower in his hand and throws it at LEAH.*]

GOLIATH: I'm going to get you, Evans.

DAVID: Why? I haven't done anything!

[*GOLIATH goes.*]

DAVID: [*whiningly*] He's bigger than me, Leah!

LEAH: Are you afraid he'll bully you?

DAVID: Yeah.

LEAH: God, David! Just stand up to him!

DAVID: You shouldn't take the Lord's name in vain.

LEAH: What? What d'you mean?

DAVID: You said "God".

LEAH: So what? You shouldn't let him frighten you! Being scared is well tight.

[*Lights down.*]

SCENE FOUR

[*Playground (and its noise). DAVID is walking around despondently. He has his hands in his pockets. He looks about him nervously. After a moment, we hear GOLIATH shouting very loudly from off. (Maybe this should be amplified in some way.)*]

GOLIATH: [*off*] Evans!

[*DAVID freezes. GOLIATH comes on. During the following, GOLIATH circles DAVID. Occasionally he makes a false lunge at DAVID which DAVID clumsily avoids though once or twice he catches DAVID on the side of the head before finally attacking him.*]

GOLIATH: Wimpy.

DAVID: What?

GOLIATH: You're wimpy.

DAVID: O.K.

GOLIATH: You don't mind me calling you wimpy? See? That proves it!

DAVID: Not really.

GOLIATH: You calling me a liar?

DAVID: No. It's just I thought you called me A wimpy.

GOLIATH: So what? What if I did call you A wimpy?

DAVID: I wouldn't like it.

GOLIATH: Why?

DAVID: 'Cos a wimpy's a burger.

GOLIATH: [*ironically*] Oh, pardon me! I suppose you're a veggie!

DAVID: What? I don't get it.

GOLIATH: A veggie. You don't eat meat.

DAVID: But I wasn't thinking of eating myself.

GOLIATH: [*nastily*] Don't get funny with me, you drong! Anyway, Wimpy's make veggie burgers. You better stay away from Leah.

DAVID: Why?

GOLIATH: 'Cos I'm telling you to. She shouldn't be going out with a pansy.

DAVID: A pansy?

GOLIATH: Yeah. You're a pansy. You love Jesus.

DAVID: So?

GOLIATH: You do! You love Jesus! Oh, bloody heck! You love Jesus! Evans is a pansy! Evans is a pansy! You must be a pansy or you wouldn't love a man!

DAVID: I don't know what you're on about.

GOLIATH: I'm on about loving a man! That's what I'm on about.

DAVID: I don't love a man! I love Jesus.

GOLIATH: Oh! What's the difference?

DAVID: Jesus is dead.

GOLIATH: You love a dead man? Si-i-ick!

DAVID: Shurrup, Gol.

GOLIATH: Shurrup? You better not tell me to shurrup or I'll wipe that smirk off your face.

DAVID: I haven't got a smirk.

GOLIATH: Maybe you want me to give you something to smirk about. Pansy. A wimpy, veggie, pansy! God! I'd kill myself! Anyway, I HATE JESUS!

DAVID: That's O.K. You're entitled to.

GOLIATH: Oh, am I? Who's entitling me?

DAVID: Jesus himself.

GOLIATH: Jesus himself?

DAVID: Yeah. He doesn't mind if you hate him.

GOLIATH: [*angrily*] Well that just sucks! I hate people who don't hate the people who hate them!

[*GOLIATH gets hold of DAVID. (Maybe in a full nelson.) DAVID makes noises of pain.*]

DAVID: Ow! Ow!

GOLIATH: If someone hates you, you should hate them back!

DAVID: [*desperately*] But you don't get it, Gol! Jesus loves those who hate him!

GOLIATH: Well, I hate you! I hate you! So what about you?

DAVID: What about me?

GOLIATH: Do you hate me?

DAVID: No.

GOLIATH: You don't?

DAVID: No.

GOLIATH: You're not going to tell me you love me, are you?

DAVID: Leave go, Gol!

GOLIATH: Tell me!

DAVID: What?

GOLIATH: D'you love me?

DAVID: Yes!

GOLIATH: Say it!

DAVID: I love you, Gol.

[*GOLIATH throws DAVID to the floor. DAVID cries out. GOLIATH sits astride him, pushing him down.*]

GOLIATH: That's the sickest thing I've ever heard! You're a pansy! That's what you are!

DAVID: No!

GOLIATH: You are!

DAVID: No!

GOLIATH: How much money have you got?

DAVID: Nothing.

GOLIATH: Give me all you got!

DAVID: I haven't got ANY!

GOLIATH: Right! That's it! You've done it now!

[*GOLIATH raises his fist. DAVID cries out.*]

DAVID: No-o-o-o-o-o-!!!!

SCENE FIVE

[*GOLIATH'S home. GOLIATH is alone. He's talking to his father who is off. GOLIATH is terrified.*]

GOLIATH'S
FATHER: [*off*] You hear me, snake face?

GOLIATH: Yes, Dad.

FATHER: [*off*] I told you not to call me Dad! I'm not your Dad! You think I'd have ended up with a son like you? A pansy?

GOLIATH: No.

FATHER: [*off*] No what?

GOLIATH: I don't know what to call you.

FATHER: [*off*] What d'you mean you don't know what to call me?

GOLIATH: I don't know.

FATHER: [*off*] Try.

            [*Pause.*]

GOLIATH: Father?

FATHER: [*off*] You mean because father sounds more respectful than Dad? Don't insult me, you lizard!

            [*GOLIATH'S face twists up as a prelude to tears.*]

FATHER: [*off*] Come on!

GOLIATH: Step-Dad?

FATHER: [*off*] Step-Dad! Ha, ha! "Happy Christmas, son" "Happy Christmas Step-Dad"! Plonker!

            [*Silence.*]

GOLIATH: Sir?

FATHER: [*off*] Let's try it. Hey, snake face!

GOLIATH: Yes, sir?

FATHER: [*off*] D'you hear me?

GOLIATH: What?

FATHER: [*off*] I want your CD player, sound system, the lot. I'm flogging the lot.

            [*GOLIATH cries. He sniffs.*]

FATHER: [*off*] What you sniffing about?

GOLIATH: Nothing.

FATHER: [*off*] Not crying are you? Not a poof?

GOLIATH: No.

FATHER: [*off*] We got no money. We gotta get fed. So that's it.

            [*Silence.*]

FATHER: [*off*] Hey, geek.

GOLIATH: What?

FATHER: [*off*] Get it. Get the stuff. I can't keep this bloke waiting.

[*GOLIATH sniffs.*]

GOLIATH: O.K.

FATHER: [*off*] Wait a minute! Wait a minute! Are you crying?

GOLIATH: No.

FATHER: [*off*] You are! You're crying, you snivelling little adder! Come here! Come here so I can give you a wallop. Give you something to cry about.

GOLIATH: [*wringing hands*] N..no...Da...sir...

FATHER: [*off*] Come here, you slimy git!

[*GOLIATH goes off to his FATHER, crying. After a moment we hear him being hit. GOLIATH cries out tearfully.*]

GOLIATH: [*off*] No! No! Stop it! Please!

[*Lights down.*]

SCENE SIX

[*The roof of a block of flats. DAVID is squatting, looking over. He has a black eye. (Two black eyes?) In his hands he has a large stone or brick. Near him is his guitar. He is poised, waiting to drop the stone. After a moment, LEAH comes on.*]

LEAH: David! What are you doing?

DAVID: Leah! What you doing here?

LEAH: I asked first.

DAVID: What?

LEAH: I asked you first: What you doing with that stone?

DAVID: Nothing.

LEAH: Nothing yet, no. Because you haven't dropped it.
           Yet.

           [*Silence.*]

LEAH: David!

DAVID: What?

LEAH: What are you going to do with that stone? Don't
           tell me you're going to drop it!

           [*Silence.*]

LEAH: Flipping heck, David! Answer me!

DAVID: Leave me alone!

LEAH: No!

DAVID: I'm going to drop it on Goliath!

LEAH: You can't! That's well criminal!

DAVID: Look at my face! Look at my eyes!

LEAH: But if you drop that on him you'll kill him! You'll
           squash him!

DAVID: It's not a very big stone.

LEAH: It doesn't matter! You're dropping it from a great
           height! It'll get faster and faster until it's like
           something much bigger than itself.

DAVID: I just want to teach him a lesson.

LEAH: You'll just flatten his head! You want to get him
           back because he hit you?

DAVID: Yeah!

LEAH: Like an eye for an eye and a tooth for a tooth?

DAVID: Yeah.

LEAH: I thought you were a Christian.

DAVID: Yeah. So?

LEAH: Well that's not very Christian. If you were a Christian, you'd turn the other cheek.

DAVID: What d'you mean? Let him hit me again?

LEAH: Yes!

DAVID: Anyway, he had me pinned down. I couldn't've turned my cheek even if I'd wanted to. He was hitting both cheeks as it was. Ssssh! I can hear him! In the hallway.

[*DAVID gets poised again. LEAH puts her arms around his neck and pulls him back.*]

LEAH: Don't, David! Don't.

DAVID: Gerroff, Leah! Gerroff me! I'll miss him!

[*DAVID falls back, losing his hold on the stone which, nevertheless, doesn't fall over the edge. He gets up again and looks over.*]

DAVID: He's gone!

[*Silence.*]

LEAH: You wouldn't've done it.

DAVID: I would have.

LEAH: You would have wanted to kill him? You must be well sick! Tell me if you wanted to kill him, David, 'cos I don't want to go with a murderer.

[*Pause.*]

DAVID: 'Course I didn't.

LEAH: It's dangerous. You shouldn't play with stones like that.

DAVID: Leave off, Leah. I'm not a kid.

LEAH: No, you're not a kid, but you're acting like a drip.

[*Silence.*]

DAVID

LEAH: Sing me a song.

DAVID: I don't feel like it.

LEAH: Come on!

DAVID: I can't think of anything.

LEAH: Just play a tune.

[*DAVID picks up a guitar. He plays a tune. After a moment, GOLIATH comes on.*]

GOLIATH: So! What you doing up here?!

[*Silence. They look at GOLIATH with shock. DAVID stops playing. GOLIATH snatches DAVID'S guitar from him. GOLIATH holds guitar over the edge.*]

GOLIATH: Shall I drop it?

L & D: [*together*] No! No!

GOLIATH: What will you give me not to?

DAVID: Anything!

GOLIATH: What?

DAVID: My cheek?

GOLIATH: What cheek?

DAVID: I'll give you my other cheek.

GOLIATH: What d'you mean? Your bum cheek?

LEAH: He means he'll turn the other cheek.

GOLIATH: But what's the point? I can take it anyway if I want.

[*GOLIATH looks over.*]

GOLIATH: Ooo, look. There's Terry Jones.

[*GOLIATH picks up the stone and drops it over. He looks after it.*]

GOLIATH: Missed! If I'd've got him I'd've said it was you.

	Got any money?
DAVID:	No.
LEAH:	I got some.
GOLIATH:	I don't want your money. I want his.
DAVID:	I haven't got any!!
GOLIATH:	Well I'll have to keep this then, won't I? Until you get some. [*pause*] Tara.
	[*GOLIATH goes taking DAVID'S guitar.*]
DAVID:	What am I going to do now?
	[*DAVID begins to cry.*]
DAVID:	I'll never get it back!
LEAH:	You don't have to cry about it! What good will that do?
DAVID:	I can't stand it any more.
LEAH:	You've just got to stand up to him!
DAVID:	That's what I wanted to do.
LEAH:	It's not standing up to him to drop a brick on his head!
DAVID:	That's only because you say so!
LEAH:	That's only because it's true!
DAVID:	To stand up to him doesn't necessarily mean that I've got to stand next to him; face to face...
	[*DAVID'S tearful face is up against LEAH'S.*]
LEAH:	Get your face out of MY face!
DAVID:	It means doing something to him that stops him from doing what he was doing to you!
LEAH:	Well if you know so much about it why don't you DO something about it?!

DAVID

[*DAVID gets up.*]

DAVID: I will! Only this time I'll make sure that you don't stop me!

[*DAVID rushes off.*]

LEAH: David!

[*Lights down.*]

SCENE SEVEN

[*ELIJAH'S room. ELIJAH is sitting cross-legged. He is chanting a mantra. DAVID is sitting in front of him still sniffing from his crying.*]

ELIJAH: Love will never die. Love will never die. Love will never die. Ommm! Love will never die. Love will never die.

[*Silence.*]

ELIJAH: Sorry, but I had to finish my mantra. That's what that's called. That chanting. A mantra. What's the matter? What you crying about?

DAVID: Goliath nicked my guitar.

ELIJAH: [*carefully, slowly*] "Goliath nicked my guitar". [*pause*] "Goliath nicked my guitar".

DAVID: What?

ELIJAH: Sssshhh!

[*ELIJAH closes his eyes. He is deep in thought.*]

ELIJAH: Close your eyes.

DAVID: What for?

ELIJAH: Just close your eyes!

[*DAVID closes his eyes.*]

ELIJAH: Right. Let's do it together. Say it together. And THINK. But think DEEPLY. Let the words roll around your head.

DAVID: What words?

ELIJAH: "Goliath nicked my guitar" [*pause*] Ready?

DAVID: This is daft.

ELIJAH: Daft? Right. Go on. Get out.

DAVID: O.K. I'll do it!

ELIJAH: This is TRAINING, man!

DAVID: O.K.

ELIJAH: Let's start again. Close your eyes.

[*They close their eyes.*]

ELIJAH: Right. [*pause*] Breathe deep.

[*They both breathe deeply.*]

ELIJAH: Here we go.

TOGETHER: Goliath nicked my guitar. Goliath nicked my guitar. Goliath nicked my guitar. Goliath nicked my guitar. Goliath nicked my guitar. Goliath nicked my guitar. Goliath nicked my guitar.

ELIJAH: Stop. [*pause*] Anything?

DAVID: What?

ELIJAH: Any meaning?

DAVID: What?

ELIJAH: Any deep, hidden meaning coming to you? Anything deep down in the bottom bed-rock of the words coming to you?

DAVID: No. Other than I'm going to get killed. And Goliath can't even play.

ELIJAH: O.K. Let's throw an OM in. Ready?

DAVID: Yeah. [*pause*] Ommmm. And you!

TOGETHER: Ommmm! Goliath nicked my guitar. Goliath nicked my guitar. Goliath nicked my guitar. Goliath nicked my guitar. Goliath nicked my guitar. Goliath nicked my guitar. Goliath nicked my guitar.

ELIJAH: Stop! [*pause*] Anything?

DAVID: No.

ELIJAH: Oh well.

DAVID: I'm still going to get killed.

ELIJAH: Yeah. It's a drag man. It's a drag. [*pause*] I'm not into Rasta any more.

DAVID: You're not?

ELIJAH: No.

DAVID: What are you?

ELIJAH: I'm not sure yet. There's a bit of Buddhism in there, but I was just finding the whole thing a bit head banging. I'm trying out these mantras now. I need time. And I need a tune. Give us a tune on my guitar.

[*David gets guitar.*]

DAVID: What you want?

ELIJAH: Something soft. Quiet. I've got to think.

[*DAVID plays something quietly.*]

ELIJAH: You see, the whole thing about religion is it's a useful thing to experiment with because it makes you THINK. Not being able to think is like having a guitar you can't play. You should feel sorry for Goliath. He can't play a guitar and he doesn't experiment with religion so he can't THINK. What's he got? He's what's called a Philistine.

DAVID: What's that?

ELIJAH: Well, strictly speaking it's someone who's got no art. Can't do anything artistic; doesn't like anything artistic. In his case it's just because he is the beast Goliath. He probably thinks — if he thinks at all — that he's a really cool dude. But if you don't know anything; if you can't even think about anything then you don't know what to do. So religion can help you think about things so that you know how to act. To solve your problem. But it's not the solution. You are.

[*DAVID stops playing.*]

DAVID: Me? How?

ELIJAH: Think!

[*Silence.*]

ELIJAH: What you doing?

DAVID: Thinking.

ELIJAH: No, no, no! You can't just think. You've got to have a focus!

[*Pause. ELIJAH has taken up a harmonica that DAVID doesn't see. ELIJAH suddenly plays a very loud blues riff that startles DAVID.*]

DAVID: Flipping heck, Lije!

[*ELIJAH holds up harmonica.*]

ELIJAH: THAT [*harmonica*] is going to get you your guitar back.

DAVID: How? I've got to stand up to him first.

ELIJAH: I know that! Obviously. It means that if the harmonica is going to get it back it's also going to let you stand up to him.

DAVID: How?

ELIJAH: I'm not going to tell you that! You'll have to figure it out for yourself. But I'll give you a clue. GOLIATH is a human being.

DAVID: I know that!

ELIJAH: So are you.

DAVID: Li-ije!

ELIJAH: Goliath is deprived. D'you get that? What it means?

DAVID: I'm not sure.

ELIJAH: [*impatiently*] Well if you're not sure ask me what it means!

DAVID: What does deprived mean? Wait a minute, I think I know that. It means he hasn't got things other people have got.

ELIJAH: It means that, yeah. It also means that no one loves him. And he's got no art! THINK! Music, human being, ART! THINKING. Thinking is called philosophy in the universities. Religion is just basic philosophy. That's all. THINK! Let's do it! MUSIC, human, thinking. Close your eyes. Deep breath.

            [*Pause.*]

ELIJAH: Ready?

DAVID: M-m-m-m.

TOGETHER:Music, human, thinking. Music, human, thinking. Music, human, thinking. Music, human, thinking. Music, human, thinking. Music, human, thinking.

ELIJAH: Stop! Next. You need some lessons. It's easy. You just blow and suck till you can feel the music! Try.

            [*ELIJAH gives harmonica to DAVID. DAVID puts harmonica to his mouth and blows tentatively.*]

ELIJAH: Suck, Davey, suck!

            [*DAVID sucks the beginning of a blues wail.*]

ELIJAH: Yes!

            [*DAVID grins broadly.*]

SCENE EIGHT

[*DAVID'S home. MOTHER is sitting at table. DAVID comes on wearing dark glasses to hide his eyes.*]

MOTHER: David! Where've you been? I missed you this morning. I know it's Saturday but you should get up earlier. Or did you get up much earlier and sneak out for some reason? Have you seen your father today? And why're you wearing those glasses? Have you been to see that Elijah again? You better not let your father see you looking like a blues brother.

DAVID: Mum!

MOTHER: What?

DAVID: When's a guitar not a guitar?

MOTHER: What?

DAVID: When's a guitar not a guitar?

MOTHER: What?

DAVID: When's a guitar not a guitar? When's a guitar not a guitar?

MOTHER: David! What's the matter? Why do you keep repeating yourself?

DAVID: It's a mantra.

MOTHER: A mantra? A mantra's a car, isn't it?

DAVID: There may be a car called a mantra but that's probably because of the engine. It keeps doing the same thing over and over again and what happens is the car goes forward in a straight line. That's what a mantra does when you say things over and over again.

MOTHER: Even when it doesn't mean anything? Like when is a guitar not a guitar? It doesn't mean anything! This is that Elijah again, isn't it? I'm going to get the police. He's brain-washing you!

DAVID: Don't be daft, Mum! When is a guitar not a guitar? When it's a harmonica!

[*DAVID quickly takes out harmonica and plays a blues wail.*]

MOTHER: Ooo! I like that! Blues.

DAVID: Do you?

MOTHER: Yes. It triggers off something deep inside. People like blues music.

DAVID: It's true then!

MOTHER: What's true?

DAVID: It's something Elijah said. He's not into Rasta any more. He's not a Rastafarian.

MOTHER: What is he now?

DAVID: I think he said he's a Buddhist.

MOTHER: I always thought Buddhists were Japanese.

DAVID: I don't think it matters where you come from. You can have a Japanese Christian.

MOTHER: Well you just listen, David. I don't want you becoming a Buddhist! You'll scare the neighbours!

[*DAVID wails on harmonica.*]

MOTHER: And I don't want any more of that either! You'll wake your father up!

FATHER: [*off*] Ruth! Is there a fire?

MOTHER: See?! Now you've woken him up!

DAVID: Sorry, Mum.

FATHER: [*off*] Ruth! I thought I heard a siren!

MOTHER: [*shouting to off*] It's nothing, Mo! It's just David. He's got a harmonica.

FATHER: [*off*] Who does he think he is? Jarvis Cocker?

DAVID: [*mischievously to MOTHER*] Yeah, I do!

MOTHER: Stop it, David! And where's your guitar?

DAVID: Um... um...

MOTHER: What?

DAVID: Um... um...

MOTHER: What's this "um"? Another one of those things?

DAVID: What things?

MOTHER: Those mantra things.

DAVID: No. That's Ommm.

MOTHER: What's "Om"?

DAVID: In a mantra you sometimes say OMM. Not UM. Like: Dad is watching telly, Dad is watching telly, OMMM, Dad is watching...

MOTHER: Shut up, David, before I wring your neck!

FATHER: [*off*] Ruth! What's going on out there? It sounds like a ruddy Buddhist monastery!

RUTH: It's nothing, love.

FATHER: [*Off*] Send that boy in here!

MOTHER: [*quietly to DAVID*] Take those glasses off, quick!

        [*She takes DAVID'S glasses off and sees his eyes. She gasps.*]

MOTHER: Oh, David! what happened?

DAVID: I fell over.

MOTHER: Don't lie! Someone's hit you.

FATHER: [*off*] Ruth!

MOTHER: Oh, God! [*to DAVID*] Sssshhh!

            [*Silence.*]

FATHER: [*off*] Ruth! Ruth!

            [*MOTHER tip-toes with DAVID to go off.*]

MOTHER: [*in an undertone*] You'd better tell me. I want to know. Something's gone wrong and I want to know. I want to know what it is.

DAVID: There's nothing wrong, Mum! I know what to do! I'm happy!

FATHER: [*off*] Ruth! I'm not having this! There's going to be trouble if that Larry Adler isn't in here within the next minute!

            [*MOTHER indicates to DAVID that he should go quietly. DAVID goes. MOTHER stands wringing her hands. Lights down.*]

SCENE NINE

[*GOLIATH'S home. GOLIATH is alone. He's banging on the guitar trying to get something out of it. He stops and cries, half out of frustration, half out of self-pity. GOLIATH has a large bruise on the side of his face.*]

GOLIATH: I can't do it! I can't do anything! I hate myself! I hate my life! I've got no friends. No one likes me. Everyone hates me. Everyone calls me names. Everyone says I don't know anything. Everyone says I'm ignorant. No one will be my girlfriend. No one will be my friend friend. I've got nothing. How come David is so clever? How come HE can play a guitar? How come he gets Leah? 'Cos he can play! Must be! That's how he gets her. 'Cos he can play music!

[*GOLIATH bangs again on guitar then slams it down wretchedly. There is a knock on the door. GOLIATH goes off. He comes back on with LEAH. He is very nervous. He walks in a way to hide the bruise from her.*]

LEAH: What will your parents say?

GOLIATH: Oh, nothing. They like me having friends round.

LEAH: Well cool. You get on alright with your Dad?

GOLIATH: Yeah. He's my step-dad.

LEAH: Why do people call him stinky? Can I sit down?

GOLIATH: Yeah. Who calls him stinky?

LEAH: Everybody. Stinky Worrell.

GOLIATH: Shurrup, Leah! Want some pop?

LEAH: Yeah. O.K.

[*GOLIATH goes off. LEAH picks up the guitar. She holds it and sings a song while pretending to play. (Maybe she actually plays a few notes.) GOLIATH comes back on. He hands LEAH a drink. He is now wearing a baseball cap pulled over to the side to hide his bruise. (LEAH has actually already seen it.)*]

GOLIATH: He fell in the canal when he was six. The canal stunk.

[*GOLIATH sits next to LEAH. She puts guitar down. They drink their pop.*]

LEAH: Gosh, Gol! That's well tight!

GOLIATH: Yeah. It's the first thing I ever remember him telling me. I 'spose he wanted to get it out of the way. He said: "If you ever hear anyone calling me Stinky, don't take any notice. It's not my fault. I

140

fell in the canal when I was six and it stunk of pooh"...

[*LEAH starts laughing but struggles to keep it to herself so that GOLIATH won't notice.*]

GOLIATH: ... and he went past a gang of his mates and they said: "Cor! You stink of Pooh! Yanta shita pantsa! Stinky stinksa pooh!" And it stuck ever since.

LEAH: What? The pooh?

[*She laughs loudly now that she has the opportunity to.*]

GOLIATH: Shurrup, Leah.

[*GOLIATH laughs despite himself.*]

LEAH: Anyway, it must have made him broadminded!

GOLIATH: Why?

LEAH: Letting you have all your friends around.

GOLIATH: Yeah. I 'spose I'm lucky. I just live a very cool life.

LEAH: Lucky your Dad once stunk of pooh!

GOLIATH: Yeah!

[*They laugh.*]

LEAH: You been practising the guitar?

GOLIATH: Yeah.

LEAH: I didn't know you could play.

GOLIATH: Oh, yeah.

LEAH: You kept that quiet.

GOLIATH: No point in bragging.

LEAH: Play us something.

GOLIATH: I... um... u... um... well you'd better go now, Leah.

LEAH: Why?

GOLIATH: Case my Dad gets back. He'll be back soon.

LEAH: So?

GOLIATH: He'll probably be drunk.

LEAH: Drunk? Does he drink a lot?

GOLIATH: All the time.

LEAH: S-i-i-i-ck, Gol.

GOLIATH: He can't help it.

LEAH: What, is he an alkie?

GOLIATH: Sort of. He gets depressed a lot.

LEAH: I'm not surprised with a name like stinky!

GOLIATH: No. He gets depressed 'cos he drinks then that makes him drink more.

LEAH: That's well sad.

GOLIATH: Yeah.

LEAH: You can't play, can you?

GOLIATH: What?

LEAH: You can't play!

GOLIATH: 'Course I can! I can play as good as David!

LEAH: So let's hear you then!

GOLIATH: No!

LEAH: Why?

GOLIATH: I told you!

LEAH: Well I'm not going!

GOLIATH: Eh?

LEAH: Not without the guitar.

GOLIATH: Is that what you came for?

LEAH: Yeah.

GOLIATH: You didn't come to see me?

LEAH: The trouble with you, Gol, is that you're like your Dad with his drinking. Because he drinks he gets depressed and that makes him drink more. Because you haven't got any friends you bully people and then you don't have any friends at all so you bully people more.

GOLIATH: But I have got friends!

LEAH: Who?

GOLIATH: Who-oo?

LEAH: Yeah!

GOLIATH: You gotta go! I think I heard my Dad!

LEAH: O.K., Gol. I tried to help but it's obviously no good. You're just going to have to face him.

GOLIATH: Face who?

LEAH: David. He's down the Reccy waiting for you.

GOLIATH: David?!! Ha, ha! What's he think he's going to do?

LEAH: He's going to face you down.

[*GOLIATH suddenly starts laughing uncontrollably. He falls to the floor holding his belly and kicking his feet into the air.*]

LEAH: It's not funny!

[*GOLIATH suddenly stops laughing and gets up.*]

GOLIATH: [*seriously*] Where is he? Is he down there now?

LEAH: Yes.

GOLIATH: Good. 'Cos I'm going to go there and smash his face into a pulp.

[*LEAH turns and goes off briskly. GOLIATH stands angrily punching his fist into his hand.*]

[*Lights down.*]

SCENE TEN

[*The Reccy. (The Showdown.) DAVID is waiting for GOLIATH. He is pacing nervously. Hidden in his hand is his harmonica.*]

GOLIATH: [*Off. Loud as before.*] Evans!

DAVID: I'm here, Gol.

[*GOLIATH comes on. He is wearing a baseball cap turned sideways to hide a bruise. They stand either side of the area and move around in a circle like gladiators facing each other.*]

GOLIATH: You phoned the undertaker? Got your coffin ready?

DAVID: Ha, ha! That's funny, Gol! It's making me laugh so much I think I'm going to pee myself!

GOLIATH: Well I hope you got your nappy on!

DAVID: Why you wearing that silly hat?

GOLIATH: Just to show you how cool I am.

[*Silence. They circle, crouching.*]

GOLIATH: You must think you've got your little Lord Jesus to help you!

DAVID: No. Don't need Him. I can do this myself.

[*Silence. They circle.*]

DAVID: You're sad, Gol.

GOLIATH: How d'you work that out?

DAVID: Because you think you're hard but you're soft. You think you're big but you're small. You think you're clever but you're thick...

GOLIATH: Shurrup!

DAVID: You think you're cool but you're a hot dog!

GOLIATH: You're right! I'm a hot dog and I'm going to bite your neck out! Drink your blood till you're dry like a plank 'cos you're thick as two short ones!

DAVID: Flipping heck, Gol! Is that the best you can do? You know what your trouble is? You want to be loved and no one loves you!

[*GOLIATH stops.*]

GOLIATH: I've had enough of your lip, Evans. I'm gonna rip it off! You ready?

DAVID: Do your best! Come and get me!

[*GOLIATH makes a move towards DAVID. DAVID suddenly puts his harmonica to his mouth and plays a very loud blues riff. GOLIATH stops in his tracks with his mouth wide open. His eyes too are wide with surprise.*]

GOLIATH: What's that?

DAVID: It's a harmonica.

[*DAVID plays again. LEAH comes on.*]

GOLIATH: How do you do it?

DAVID: It's easy. You just suck and blow.

LEAH: What you hiding under your cap, Gol?

[*GOLIATH is surprised to see LEAH.*]

GOLIATH: What d'you want?

LEAH: Come on! Let's see.

GOLIATH: There's nothing.

DAVID: What is it, Leah?

[*LEAH moves up to GOLIATH.*]

LEAH: It's a bruise.

DAVID: What?

GOLIATH: It's not! It's paint.

LEAH: It's not! I saw it earlier, Gol! It's a bruise and it looks serious.

[LEAH sneaks up behind GOLIATH. She flips his cap off.]

GOLIATH: Hey!

LEAH: See! That's well bad, Gol! It looks well serious! Who's done that? Have a look, Dave.

DAVID: Let's have a look, Gol.

GOLIATH: It's nothing, mun.

LEAH: No kid could've done that. How could they? You're the bully!

GOLIATH: Me? I'm not a bully!

LEAH: 'Course you are! You're having a go at David, aren't you? Or do you think it's not having a go?

GOLIATH: I'm just defending myself.

DAVID: Leave it out, Gol! I never started it! You nicked my guitar!

GOLIATH: Yeah. But it wasn't serious.

LEAH: So what's serious? That bruise is WELL serious!

DAVID: Can I have a look, Gol?

[DAVID comes up to GOLIATH. DAVID and LEAH examine the bruise carefully.]

LEAH: Who did it, Gol? Tell us.

DAVID: Come on. Tell us. It was your Dad, wasn't it?

GOLIATH: *[emphatically]* Step-Dad!

LEAH: He's not allowed to do that! It's against the law!

DAVID: What we going to do about it, Gol?

GOLIATH: What?

LEAH: We've got to do something. Tell someone.

GOLIATH: [*about harmonica*] Can I have a go of that?

[*Pause.*]

GOLIATH: I'll give you your guitar back.

DAVID: O.K.

GOLIATH: Give us it then.

LEAH: Not yet. We've got something to sort, first.

GOLIATH: What?

LEAH: Who're you going to tell?

[*Pause.*]

DAVID: Not scared are you, Gol?

LEAH: Yeah. 'Cos that's another sign of a bully: being a coward.

GOLIATH: Scared of what?

LEAH: Of dobbing on your old man.

GOLIATH: 'Course not!

LEAH: Is the dob on then?

GOLIATH: What's the point?

DAVID: D'you like getting decked?

GOLIATH: I didn't get decked!

LEAH: You will! And by your own Dad!

GOLIATH: STEP-Dad!

DAVID: O.K., but he's still your Dad! And no Dad should deck his kid!

[*Silence. The three look at each other intensely as though it's a stand-off.*]

GOLIATH: [*to the other two*] What?

LEAH: Well?

GOLIATH: What?

DAVID: What?!

GOLIATH: I dunno.

LEAH: What?

DAVID: You dunno what?

GOLIATH: I dunno! That's what I dunno!

LEAH: Gol, you're ignorant, aren't you?

GOLIATH: Who said?

LEAH: You said! To me!

GOLIATH: Yeah, I am.

LEAH: That's why you dunno. Because you don't know anything.

GOLIATH: Yeah!

DAVID: So if you dunno....

LEAH: You don't know that we know.

GOLIATH: Know what? [*Impatiently. About harmonica.*] What about that?

LEAH: WE know that you've got to tell somebody.

           [*Silence.*]

DAVID: Want to be friends, Gol?

GOLIATH: What, friends with you and Leah?

LEAH: .Yeah.

GOLIATH: Can I play that?

DAVID: 'Course you can.

GOLIATH: O.K. then. Yu-uy yeah. [*pause*] Yeah!

LEAH: But you've got to let us tell.

GOLIATH: Aw, flippin heck!

LEAH: You've got to!

[*Pause.*]

DAVID: Let's do a mantra.

GOLIATH: What?

DAVID: A mantra! Sit down. In a circle.

[*LEAH and DAVID sit.*]

DAVID: Come on, Gol! It's like a song!

[*GOLIATH reluctantly sits.*]

DAVID: O.K. Now we chant. Just follow me. But first, an OM.

GOLIATH: An OM? What's an OM?

DAVID: Just an OM! That's what it is! [*he does it*] OMMM. O.K.? All of us.

GOLIATH: This is daft!

DAVID: Come on!

TOGETHER: OMMMM!

DAVID: O.K. Now the chant. Follow me: Gol's gonna let us tell, Gol's gonna let us tell!

[*LEAH joins in.*]

DAVID & LEAH: Gol's gonna let us tell! Gol's gonna let us tell!

DAVID: [*to GOLIATH*] Come on!

ALL: Gol's gonna let us tell. Gol's gonna let us tell!

[*GOLIATH starts giggling.*]

DAVID: [*as LEAH continues*] Come on, Gol! Keep going!

[*The three continue with GOLIATH having some difficulty controlling himself.*]

ALL: Gol's gonna let us tell! Gol's gonna let us tell! Gol's gonna let us tell! Gol's gonna let us tell! Gol's gonna let us tell!

DAVID: Right, keep going!

[*LEAH and GOLIATH carry on.*]

DAVID: Then change it to: We're going to dob on Gol's dad; we're going to dob on Gol's dad... etc.

[*They all do it. As they're doing it, DAVID plays a wail on harmonica. DAVID joins in chanting then he hands harmonica to GOLIATH. LEAH continues to chant.*]

DAVID: [*handing harmonica*] You!

GOLIATH: [*panicking*] How?

DAVID: Just suck and blow till you feel the music!

[*GOLIATH puts harmonica to his mouth. He blows then sucks.*]

DAVID: [*happily*] Suck, Gol! Suck!

[*GOLIATH sucks deeply on harmonica and produces a bluesy wail. DAVID picks up guitar. The mantra stops as he sings:*]

DAVID: Let us sing this simple song
it is what we can do,
we will dob on anyone
whoever bullies me or you!

[*GOLIATH attempts to play along on harmonica. LEAH sings and laughs, etc.*]

DAVID: Will you do it, Gol? Will you do the dob?

GOLIATH: Yeah!

[*They play on and sing:*]

Let us play our simple tune
in the place where the bully played;

DAVID

let us sing our simple song
to show the world we're not afraid!

[*Laughter, etc.*]

[*Lights down.*]

Teacher's Notes

The plays were originally part of Spectacle Theatre's Literacy and Oracy project "Reading Between The Lines". The plays were an attempt by the Company to bring about a significant kind of learning through the use of theatre and workshops.

The Shakespeare Factory

This play and workshop was targeted at schools (Key Stage 3 & 4 — ages 14-16) and community venues. The brief the Company gave the writer was to take the three Shakespearian texts being studied at 'O' level, *Midsummer Nights Dream, Romeo & Juliet* and *Julius Caesar* and to weave them together to form a play that revealed the power of imagination and argument. Each school participated in one of the three workshops that followed the performance. The purpose of the workshop was to explore how theatre can be a force for democracy enabling us to take a greater part in our lives and the things that shape those lives. *The Shakespeare Factory* toured in the Autumn of 1993.

Moon River: The Deal

This play and workshop were targeted at Year 6 pupils studying at Key Stage 2. The brief the Company gave the writer was to explore the culture of the child and the importance of imaginative play. We shared the fact that culture is ordinary in every society and every mind. We quickly realised the potential to explore culture and imagination by focussing on a child's relationship to the American classic, *Huckleberry Finn*. The liberating quality in the play spilled over into the workshop which required the participating pupils to unlock their own imaginative skills by creating two rooms that the central character inhabited. A teachers' resource pack was provided to continue work in the classroom. The play was toured in Spring and Summer 1993.

David

David was targeted to pupils studying at Key Stage 2 (years 5, 6, 7). Spectacle Theatre wanted to re-look at the stories we had known since our childhood. Many of these were biblical stories, powerful stories that had begun to lose their power through familiarity. We asked the writer to use these stories to create a play that presented a positive approach to dealing with bullying whilst sensitively exploring the issues behind what makes a bully. *David* is based on the biblical story of David and Goliath and is set in a modern-day Valleys community. *David* toured during the Spring of 1996.

Steve Davis

Acknowledgements

The author wishes to thank Steve Davis and Spectacle Theatre Company who commissioned all of these plays. The author also acknowledges the financial assistance of the Arts Council of Wales.

About the Author

Dic Edwards was born in Cardiff and educated at Lampeter University and the University of Wales at Aberystwyth.

He has had fifteen full-length lays produced throughout the UK including, most recently, *Casanova Undone* and *Wittgenstein's Daughter* at Glasgow's Citizens Theatre and The White Bear in London, *Utah Blue* at The Point in Cardiff and *Lola Brecht* (Castaway Touring Co.) — UK Tour.

He has also written two opera libretti for Mark Dornford-May which were produced at Broomhill International Opera Festival in Kent.

He has just completed a new play, *idiots!*, and is currently working on a five year Oracy and Literacy project with Spectacle Theatre Co.

The author's published plays include: *At The End Of The Bay* (Spectrum Press, 1982), *3 Plays* and *Wittgenstein's Daughter*, both with Oberon Books Ltd., London and *Utah Blue* (Made In Wales, 1995). He is also a published poet.

Dic Edwards has three children and lives with his wife Gwenda and daughter Natalie in Aberaeron on the west coast of Wales.